Successful Long-Term Weight Training

Steven J. Fleck, Ph.D.

MASTERS PRESS
NTC/Contemporary Publishing Group

Library of Congress Cataloging-in-Publication Data

Fleck, Steven J.,
Successful long-term weight training / Steven J. Fleck.
p. cm.
Includes bibliographical references (p.)
ISBN 1-57028-194-7 (trade)
1. Weight training. 2. Bodybuilding. I. Title.
GV546.F56 1998
796.41—dc21 97-52773
CIP

The author and publisher assume no responsibility for any injury that may occur as a result of attempting to do any of the movements, techniques, or exercises described in this book. These exercises require strenuous physical activity and a physical examination is advisable before starting this or any other exercise program.

Cover design by Todd Petersen
Interior design by Holly Kondras

Published by Masters Press
A division of NTC/Contemporary Publishing Group, Inc.
4255 West Touhy Avenue, Lincolnwood (Chicago), Illinois 60646-1975 U.S.A.

Printed in the United States of America
International Standard Book Number: 1-57028-194-7
99 00 01 02 03 04 CU 18 17 16 15 14 13 12 11 10 9 8 7 6 5 4 3 2 1

Contents

Preface

Weight training is a very popular fitness activity. This is in large part because it is fun to do and has many health and fitness benefits. The many benefits can be attained at virtually any point in your life. So no doubt the popularity of weight training will continue to grow. Yet many people who train hard do not reap the maximum benefits. This is in large part because they make some mistakes when putting together their weight training program and when actually doing it. Some of these mistakes simply mean that the person will not get the maximum benefits of weight training. Others could result in injury. The goal of this book is to empower you, so that you do not make these mistakes but do reap the maximum benefits with the least amount of effort from weight training.

The book is made up of three parts. All of these parts are necessary in order for you to get the most out of your weight training with the least amount of effort. The first part discusses the benefits of weight training, the second discusses how to put together a weight training program that meets your individual needs and goals, and the third part discusses proper weight training technique and gives example weight training programs to meet various fitness needs.

Chapter 1 discusses the health and fitness benefits of weight training and what health benefits weight training will not bring about. This information is needed to put together a program that will produce the desired benefits with the least amount of effort. Chapter 2 describes how muscles work. This information allows a better understanding of how to most easily reap the many benefits of weight training.

The five chapters that follow are the meat and potatoes of how to put together a program that meets your goals and needs. Chapter 3 describes different types of weight training equipment that can be used in a training program. If you know how equipment works, it is easy to use it properly and safely. Chapter 4 discusses weight room safety and etiquette. No matter how good the program is put together, if it is not safe, you will not get the maximum benefits from it. Chapter 5 shows you how to put together a program that meets your goals and needs. Discussed are such things as how to choose exercises and how many repetitions and sets to do. Chapter 6 completes the discussion on how to put together your training program by describing how all the program choices you make work together to get you to your fitness goals. How to vary your program over a year or a lifetime to continue to reach your training goals is also described. Chapter 7 discusses the importance of keeping a training log and how to use the information in it to help you continually vary your program so that you do not waste valuable training time, but get the most out of the training you do.

The last two chapters discuss the tools of any weight training, the exercises, and gives sample programs to help you reach your fitness goals. Chapter 8 describes and gives illustrations of proper technique for the most popular fitness weight training exercises. Many lifters do not use good exercise technique, which is needed to safely attain fitness goals. The ninth and final chapter gives samples of the most popular fitness weight training programs. These programs can be used to reach your fitness goals, or they can be customized using the information in this book to meet your individual fitness needs.

The information contained in this book will allow you to put together an individualized weight training program that meets your needs and goals. In essence, you will be your own personal trainer, and who else knows your fitness needs and goals better than you?

Good luck and good training.

Acknowledgments

I would like to first thank all the fitness enthusiasts, coaches, and athletes who shared their weight training programs and ideas with me. Through the years these ideas have been an invaluable source of information. I would especially like to thank Bill Kraemer for his friendship, both personal and professional, over the years. A special thanks to Butch Cooper and Holly Kondras for giving me the opportunity to complete this book.

Finally, a special thanks to Maelu, my wife, for putting up with the hours of time needed to write, rewrite, and finally proofread this book. Your patience and support can never be repaid.

Chapter *One*

Why Weight Train?

So you are thinking about starting a weight training program because of all the good things you have heard it can do for you. But what exercises should you do, how many times do you need to do them, and how often do you need to train to reap all the benefits?

Perhaps you are already doing a weight training program but not making any progress. You are thinking about quitting, but quitting is not a good idea because you will start to lose all the physical benefits that your weight training has produced to date. And not starting means you will never have the chance to reap any of the benefits.

What do you do? Call a personal trainer and pay $50 per training session, or maybe buy a book? After reading the book, you lose interest or learn how to do a weight training session that is supposed to fit everyone. But when you discover that one-size-fits-all program does not meet your individual needs or goals, you quit anyway. So the only weight you lift is the book to get it out of your way.

The information in this book will make it simple for you to understand your body's reaction to weight training and to start a program or alter your present program to bring about your desired fitness gains over the long haul. Once you set the goals of your weight training program, this book will help you put together a program for you as an individual—rather than simply saying, "Here is a program, do as I say."

When you hear all of the expressions, such as "looking toned" or "buff" or having "awesome abs," you must remember that these are specific goals. Not all weight training programs will result in the accomplishment of these goals. The appearance we associate with certain expressions like "hard body" are only achieved by a certain type of weight training program. The information in this book will help you accomplish your goals. It will also help you understand the physiology of weight training and use that knowledge to design a program specifically for you, not pigeonhole you and everyone else into the same weight training program.

Weight training is one of the most popular forms of fitness exercise because it results in many positive benefits for your health and well-being. All you have to do is go to any good health club to see how popular it is. Yet how often have you gone to the gym and seen everyone being led around by a personal trainer and being told to do the exact same workout of three sets of 10 repetitions of every exercise? Or seen an individual who looks like Mr. or Ms. Universe telling a novice lifter to start out with four strip sets followed by some heavy negatives to get some size? Then there are the people who look really lost and are putting weight plates on the storage rack of a machine and wondering why the exercise is not getting more difficult. So you say to yourself, none of this is for me.

What you need is your own personal weight training program. This is really much simpler to do than you think. All you need to know are the goals of your program, such as increased muscle size, toning, or increased strength. The only other information you need is how many sets, repetitions, and days per week you need to lift in order to reach your goals. As time goes on, you can simply change the program if your goals change. For example, at age 20 a man may want big arms and has the time to train to reach that goal. At age 40 he may be more interested in health benefits and no longer have two hours a day to train. Both of these goals are achievable, but the program will be quite different.

Weight training does cause many changes in your body that are beneficial for your health and appearance. There are also some desirable changes in your body that weight training is not good at bringing about. Knowing what weight training is good at changing and the things that weight training is not so good at changing will help you plan the best possible weight training program to meet your needs and fitness goals.

Benefits of Weight Training

Many people weight train because it makes them feel energized and look better. Weight training does make you look better by toning muscles. It also burns calories resulting in loss of body fat and increases muscle size if that is what you want your weight training to accomplish. There are, however, other health and fitness benefits that are not so easily seen.

Bone Density

Loss of bone density due to aging used to be thought of as a major problem only for women. It is becoming clear, however, that this is a health concern for men as well. Loss of bone density, which we usually associate with the aged, is actually a cumulative disease. Any physical activity that is weight bearing can result in an increase of bone density or at least slow the loss of bone density as we age. Weight training is a weight bearing activity and so can increase or at least slow the loss of bone density.

For any change in bone density to occur, the bone must be exposed to weight bearing. Thus it can be expected that walking and running could result in an increase in bone density in the legs and hips but have little effect on the arms and upper body. During these activities, the bones of the upper body are not bearing any weight. During weight training, however, both the upper and lower body can be caused to bear weight. So weight training can have an effect on bone density in both the upper and lower body. This is a unique aspect of weight training that is sometimes overlooked when bone density is considered.

Loss of bone density is cumulative with time. The best approach for not having a fracture when one is older is a two-pronged attack. First, physical activity should be performed during the younger years when one is growing. Bone density increases up until about age 30, then it starts to gradually decrease. One goal of physical activity before age 30 is to make your bone density and bone mass as great as possible. This means that after 30, when your bone density starts to decrease, it will not reach that critical level where fractures are a real problem until, let's say, age 100. At that point bone density will not be a concern for most of us. This is equivalent to putting money in the bank with the goal of having enough money saved to last your entire retirement.

Do not think that you have missed the opportunity to do something for your bones. It is never too late to do weight training to increase bone density or to at least slow down a loss in bone density. This is the second prong of the approach for not having a fracture when you are older. After age 30, weight training can still increase bone density or at least slow the loss of bone density so that, again, a fracture is not a problem in the average lifespan. This is like being frugal with your retirement money; do not spend it too fast so that you run out before your retirement is over. The bottom line is, weight training can be used as an effective tool against loss of bone density during virtually all stages of our lives.

Controlling Body Weight

Controlling body weight is another reason to weight train. Weight training, like all physical activity, burns calories, which helps in decreasing total body weight over time. But the most important way weight training can help control body weight over the course of a lifetime is by maintaining or even increasing your muscle mass. We all have wondered at the amount of food some kids can eat and not gain weight or get fat. This is in part because they are still growing and in part because they have a large muscle mass compared with their body fat or total body weight. It takes calories to keep muscle alive even when it is not being used, but it takes only a few calories to keep fat alive. Muscle burns more calories than fat even while it is resting or not being used. This means that if a high percentage of your total body weight is muscle, you can eat more calories and not gain weight. If a smaller percentage of your total body weight is muscle, you have to eat fewer calories not to gain weight.

Let's say there are two people of the same body weight and eating the same diet and total number of calories, but one has a greater muscle mass than the other. This means that the one with a smaller muscle mass is carrying around more fat weight. Again let's say that the person with more muscle weight can burn 50 more calories per day just because he has more muscle. Fifty calories per day does not seem like much, but let's do a little math. There are 3,600 calories in a pound of fat. So in 72 days the person with the smaller muscle mass will gain a pound of fat (3,600 calories divided by 50 calories/day = 72 days). In one year, this person will gain about 5 pounds of fat, in two years 10 pounds, and in three years 15 pounds of fat. This is how many people gain fat weight. You just do not get fat overnight; it takes time. Maintaining your muscle mass as you age can have a very large impact on your body's makeup.

As they age, most people lose muscle mass. However, many people lose muscle mass much more quickly because they choose to live a sedentary lifestyle. If you are sedentary, you will lose muscle much faster than an individual who leads an active lifestyle. This results in burning fewer calories, not only because of a lack of activity but also because of a muscle mass loss and fat weight gain. Weight training is the most effective way to increase or maintain muscle mass, which helps to burn more calories even at rest and so keeps your fat weight from increasing as you age.

Increased Strength

Increased strength is a weight training benefit desired by many people. An increase in strength has many potential effects on our daily lives and recreation activities. Increased strength can make it possible to hit a softball or golf ball farther. It can also make it easier to carry that backpack while on vacation. One benefit of increasing or maintaining strength as we age is maintaining our ability to perform simple daily life activities like climbing stairs, carrying groceries, and getting out of a chair. Increased strength may also help prevent falls—a major factor in preventing fractures in the aged. It is now apparent that weight training can increase strength in virtually anyone of any age who trains on a consistent basis.

Increased Performance

Increased performance in activities like running and jumping is something many people would like to get out of weight training. This is why weight training is so popular among athletes. They really do not care about how strong they are, but can they hit a ball harder, throw it farther, run faster, or jump higher? This is the bottom line for most athletes. There is a lot of empirical evidence and sport science research that supports the notion that weight training can increase sports performance. So if you want to hit that golf ball farther or that tennis ball faster, weight training is for you.

Muscle Size

An increase in muscle size is a characteristic that many people desire; however, some people, women in particular, do not find this to be a desirable characteristic. A properly designed weight training program can result in either an increase in muscle size and strength or an increase in strength with little or no change in muscle size. The fact that there are two possible outcomes emphasizes the need for a weight training program put together to meet your goals as an individual.

Appearance

A side benefit to maintaining your muscle mass is that you look better and thinner. Muscle is denser than fat. This is why muscular people tend to sink in water but a chubbier person tends to float. The greater density of muscle means that a pound of muscle actually takes up less space or volume than a pound of fat. So if two people weigh the same but one has greater muscle mass, he or she will actually look thinner than the person with a smaller muscle mass. This is why in many weight training studies, especially involving

Weight Training Benefits

- √ Increase strength
- √ Increase power
- √ Increase or maintain bone density
- √ Increase sports performance
- √ Increase or maintain muscle size
- √ Decrease percent body fat
- √ Control total body weight

women, there is no change in total body weight but a decrease in arm or leg circumference. What happened is, the people gained some muscle mass and lost some fat. Because muscle is denser than fat, they appeared to be thinner. So be concerned with what your body is made up of and not just with how much you weigh.

Weight training can accomplish the things discussed above. If these are things you would like to see changed in your body, then weight training should be a part of your fitness program. Now let's look at some things that weight training is not so good at changing so we can get a total picture of what you can expect from a weight training program.

What Weight Training Is Not Good at Changing

Weight training is an excellent type of physical conditioning and should be a major part of your conditioning program, but it is not the answer for everything. In general, weight training is not good at changing things that are positively affected by aerobic or endurance training.

Endurance

Circuit weight training, quickly moving from one to the next, is the type of weight training that has the greatest effect on cardiovascular endurance or maximal oxygen consumption. Maximal oxygen consumption is many times measured when running on a treadmill and is considered one of the best indicators of cardiovascular fitness and endurance. Circuit weight training increases maximal oxygen consumption by about 5 to 8 percent in untrained men and women, respectively, in 12 to 20 weeks of training. In the same length of time, traditional running or cycling cardiovascular training increases maximal oxygen consumption by 15 to 25 percent. So traditional cardiovascular training increases endurance three to five times more than circuit weight training.

Traditional heavy weight training using heavy weights and small numbers of repetitions per set has almost no effect on maximal oxygen consumption. So if you want to increase your endurance using weight training, do a circuit-type program. If you really want to improve your endurance, however, you need to do some cardiovascular training as part of your total fitness program.

Heart Rate and Blood Pressure

Weight training does not decrease the resting heart rate or blood pressure. A decrease in the resting heart rate is associated with an increase in cardiovascular endurance. Weight training may decrease the resting heart rate slightly over time. It may also decrease your resting blood pressure slightly if you are hypertensive (i.e., have elevated resting blood pressure). In most cases, however, weight training will have little or no effect on the resting heart rate or blood pressure. It is important to note that weight training will not make you hypertensive as was once believed.

Cholesterol Profile

Weight training will not affect your cholesterol profile—another characteristic that is usually positively changed by cardiovascular training. Normally, several changes in your cholesterol or blood lipid profile, which can occur due to physical training, are viewed as positive changes. A decrease in total cholesterol is a good change. Total cholesterol tends to increase as we age. How much of this increase is really caused by aging and how much is due to a bad diet and inactivity is being looked at now by scientists. An increase in high-density lipoprotein (HDL) is viewed as a good change because HDL does not tend to stick to blood vessel walls and clog them. A decrease in low-density lipoprotein (LDL), or the "bad cholesterol," is good because LDL does tend to stick to blood vessel walls and clog them. Cardiovascular, or endurance, training has a positive effect on your blood cholesterol profile, and this is a major reason that endurance-type exercise should be a part of your total fitness program.

Flexibility

It was once thought that weight training would make you muscle-bound, or inflexible. Research, however, shows us that weight training for the most part has no effect on flexibility and may even increase flexibility at some joints. It is a good idea to move through the full range of motion of each weight training exercise (i.e., move as far as possible up and down in most exercises) to promote an increase in flexibility. However, stretching and flexibility training should also be a part of your total fitness program.

Weight training should be a part of your fitness program because it is a good tool to bring about some very important health and fitness changes in your body. It is not, however, the best tool to bring about all positive health and fitness changes. So in addition to weight training, some cardiovascular and flexibility training should be a part of your fitness program. If the changes that weight training is good at bringing about are part of what you desire, then weight training should be a major part of your fitness program. You now know what weight training is good at and not good at in relation to fitness and health changes. In the next chapter the manner in which muscles work is discussed. This is important information, because if you understand how muscles work, then you can better understand weight training.

What Weight Training Is Not Good at Changing

- √ Cardiovascular endurance
- √ Resting heart rate and blood pressure
- √ Total blood cholesterol
- √ High-density lipoprotein (HDL)
- √ Low-density lipoprotein (LDL)
- √ Flexibility

Chapter *Two*

How Muscles and Weight Training Work

You do not have to be a physiologist to understand how muscle works. Understanding how muscle works is important to understanding how weight training affects your body. Muscle is made up mostly of protein and, like all tissue, has the needed cell structures to keep it alive, grow, and repair itself if damaged. What is unique about the protein in muscle is its ability to shorten and develop force.

Because muscle can shorten and develop force, you can move your limbs. Muscle provides the force to move your skeletal joints. The shortening of muscle in gym lingo is called *positive work,* and in muscle physiology lingo it is known as a *concentric* action. In most weight training exercises, when you lift the weight the muscle shortens, or does positive work.

Muscle is built to shorten and develop force. This has several important implications for weight training and all daily movement. If muscle is built to shorten and develop force, you are probably wondering how you get the weight down in an exercise after lifting it. Muscle can also fight being lengthened. It can briefly stay at the same length, relax and be pulled to a slightly longer length, and then briefly stay at the slightly longer length. This process continues until the weight is lowered back to the starting position in most exercises. If muscle could not "fight" being lengthened after you lifted the weight, and you chose to relax your muscles, the weight would fall because of the force of gravity.

Let's look at an example to make this clearer. You are doing an elbow curl, which involves the muscles on the front of your upper arm, or the biceps muscle group. As you start the exercise, the elbow is straight. This means that the biceps is at its longest possible length. You decide to lift the weight. The biceps shorten and develop force and the weight is lifted until the elbow is completely bent. Now if you relax the biceps, gravity will pull the weight down, the elbow will start to straighten and the biceps will be pulled to a longer length. The only way you can lower the weight in a controlled fashion is for your biceps to fight being lengthened by the force of gravity. This fighting is termed *negative work* in gym lingo or an *eccentric* action by a physiologist (see Figure 1).

Let's look at this a little further. If the biceps could shorten and push on the bones to straighten the elbow, you would not need the muscle on the back of your arm called the triceps. The triceps can do the same things as the biceps except when it shortens, the elbow is straightened. As all muscles can only shorten and develop force, you must have a muscle or muscles on both sides of all your joints. If muscles could shorten, or pull on the bones of a joint, and lengthen of their own accord, or actually push on the bones, then one muscle could both bend and straighten the joint. You could do all the movements you can now with half the muscles.

Besides shortening (positive work) and fighting being lengthened (negative work), you can also choose to have a muscle develop force with no change in length. Let's say you are lifting a weight and decide to hold it at a certain joint position. If the weight is not too heavy you can choose to do this. When a muscle is developing force but no visible movement takes place it is called an *isometric*, or static, muscle action.

When you lift the weight in the leg press exercise, the quadriceps, hamstrings, and gluteals are all doing positive muscle actions. When the weight is lowered or held stationary, the same muscles are all doing negative or isometric muscle actions. During the lifting and lowering of a weight, the same muscles are being used. This is true for all normal weight training exercises.

So your muscles are built to do three major types of actions: isometric (no movement), positive (shortening), and negative (fighting being lengthened). During which of these can you develop the most force? In general, a muscle can develop the most force in a negative action,

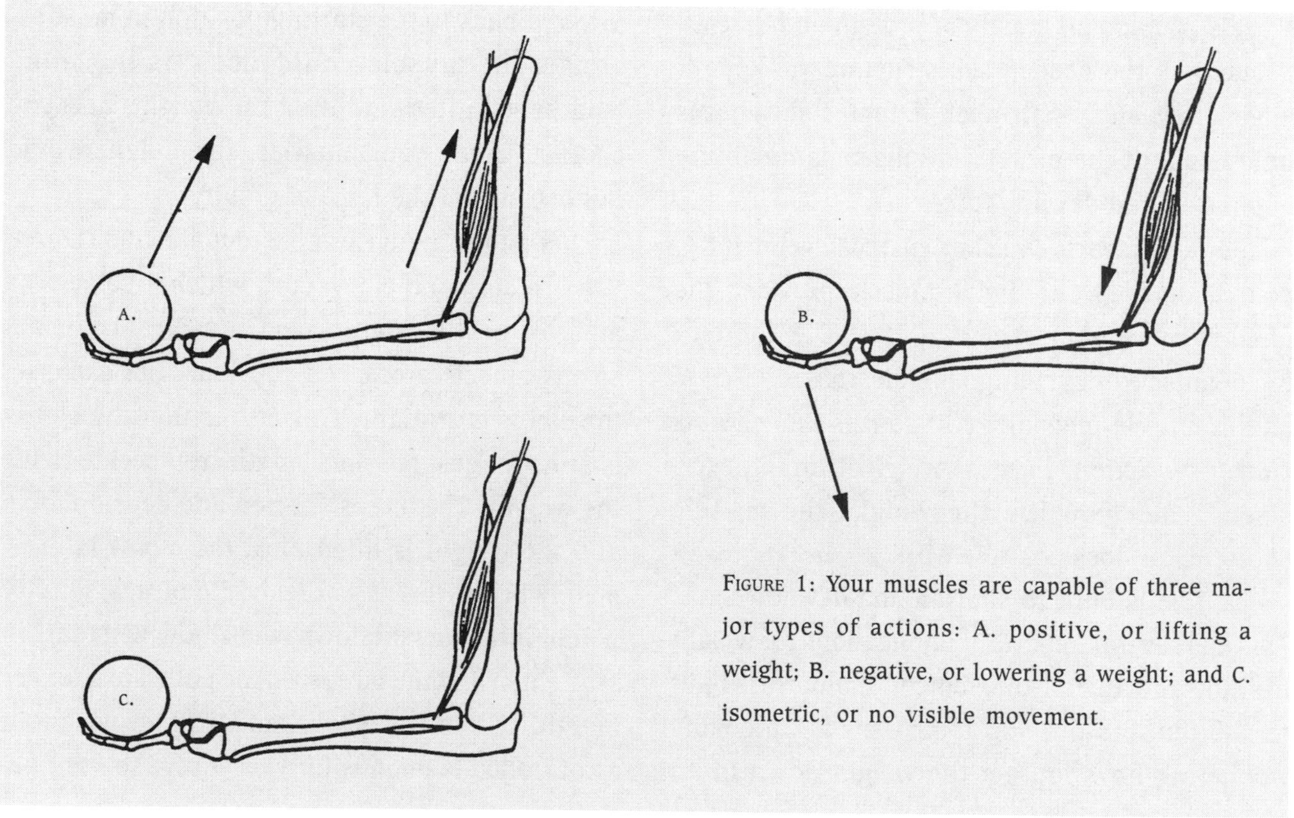

Figure 1: Your muscles are capable of three major types of actions: A. positive, or lifting a weight; B. negative, or lowering a weight; and C. isometric, or no visible movement.

followed by an isometric action and then by a positive action. This is why you can lower more weight (negative action) than you can lift (positive action) in most weight training exercises. This also means that in normal weight training (lifting and lowering the same amount of weight), the weight being used is limited by how much you can lift during the positive portion of the exercise.

Because you can lower more weight than you can lift, more force is developed by the muscle when lowering the heaviest possible weight. This is why negative weight training, or lowering more weight than you lift, results in more soreness than normal weight training. You do not instantly have more muscle as soon as you start to lower a weight, so if you lower more weight than you can lift, the same amount of muscle must develop more force. This results in more minute damage to the muscle, and so there is more soreness with heavy negative weight training.

Overloading a Muscle

Overloading a muscle refers to asking it to do more work or develop more force than it presently can do easily. Overloading is a major stimulus to change in a muscle, which can result in increased strength or size. You must overload the muscle if you expect an increase in strength to take place. You can overload the muscle in several ways. You can increase the weight being used to do a certain number of repetitions. (A repetition, or rep, is one complete movement in an exercise and normally includes the lifting and lowering of the weight.) If this is done, the weight should be increased by no more than 5 percent. This means that if you are using 100 pounds to do 10 reps, the weight can be increased by 5 pounds. If you are using 50 pounds to do 10 reps, the weight should only be increased by 2.5 pounds. This ensures a smooth progression in the amount of weight being used which, in turn, helps ensure maintenance of good exercise technique and helps prevent excessive soreness. The weight used is termed *intensity*, and increasing intensity is a major way to increase strength.

The intensity determines how many repetitions you can do per set. This simply means that it is impossible to do a lot of repetitions using a really heavy weight. The heaviest weight you can use to do 1 repetition of an exercise with good technique is called a *1 repetition maximum* or *1 RM*. The weight that allows 5 but not 6 repetitions with good exercise technique is a 5 RM. So an RM weight is the weight that allows x number of repetitions, but not x + 1 repetitions per set. Using an RM weight ensures that the muscle is overloaded and therefore will be stimulated to get stronger. This does not mean that you have to use an RM weight during all sets of an exercise or on all training days, but it does mean that if you expect to get stronger, you must at some point use at least close to an RM weight sometime during your training.

You can also increase the amount of work performed. The amount of work performed is termed the *volume of training* and is equivalent to the total number of repetitions done. Volume performed by a certain muscle group can be increased in several ways. First, you can do more repetitions per set. (A set is a certain number of repetitions done consecutively before the weight is put down, and you take a rest before the next set or exercise.) You can also do more sets of an exercise, or you can do more exercises that use a certain muscle group (such as standing and lying knee curls in the same workout) to increase the volume of training.

Intensity and volume of training are related. It is obvious that when doing a large number of repetitions, it is impossible to use your

1 RM weight for an exercise. Likewise, if you are going to do only a small number of repetitions, you can choose to use a heavy weight. Volume and intensity will be discussed in greater detail in Chapter 5. So you can overload a muscle either with a higher intensity or with increased volume, and overloading is the stimulus to bring about adaptations like increased strength and muscle size.

What Does Overloading Do?

When a muscle is overloaded several things that result in increased strength and muscle size occur. During the first several weeks of training, you learn how to do the exercise correctly. You learn how to best use the muscle or muscles to do the exercise. If more than one muscle is involved in the exercise, you learn how to best coordinate the muscles to do the exercise. You also learn how to best coordinate different parts of the individual muscles. All of these combine to result in a relatively quick increase in strength.

The protein in your muscle also begins to change during the first few weeks of training. Some of the types of protein in your muscle have several different subtypes. All the subtypes do the same job; however, some subtypes are a little better than others at doing certain things, like causing the muscle to shorten as quickly as possible. Such a shift is called a change in the *quality* of muscle protein. This type of change does not result in a noticeable increase in muscle size, but it does result in increased strength and power.

After the first several weeks of training, a noticeable increase in muscle size may occur. The change in size is caused by an increase in the total amount of protein in the muscle. Remember, protein makes up the machinery that allows muscle to develop force. So the more protein there is in a muscle, the more force it can develop. This is why a bigger muscle can develop more force. There are things you can do in training that can emphasize either strength with little change in muscle size or strength with muscle size. Remember, how you train will impact what characteristics you develop.

Learning how muscle works is important to understanding the use of accessory equipment such as a weight training belt and how different types of weight training equipment work. That is the subject of the next chapter.

Chapter *Three*

Weight Training Equipment

There are many types of weight training equipment and exercises. All of these pieces of equipment and exercises have certain characteristics. Knowledge about the characteristics allows you to make intelligent decisions concerning whether or not to use a certain type of exercise or equipment in your training program.

Types of Exercises

There are many weight training exercise classification schemes. One that is easy to understand yet useful characterizes exercises as single-joint or multi-joint.

Single-Joint Exercises

Single-joint exercises, as the name implies, mainly involve movement at one joint and therefore train predominantly one muscle group. These types of exercises are also called isolation exercises because they isolate and train one muscle group. Examples of single-joint exercises and the muscle group they train are as follows: knee extensions—quadriceps; knee curls—hamstrings; triceps extensions—triceps; and lateral shoulder raises—deltoids.

Because these types of exercises isolate one muscle group, they are used in rehabilitation programs. If you hurt the ligaments of your knee, you will eventually do knee extensions and knee curls for the quadriceps and hamstrings during the rehabilitation program. The ability to isolate one muscle group also makes these exercises useful for when you know of a weak muscle group involved in a movement. For example, let's say you are trying to increase your bench press ability. If you know which muscle group is the weakest while doing your bench press, you can use a single-joint exercise to strengthen this group and so increase your bench press ability. You can tell which is the weakest group in a movement because it will normally be the one that is the sorest or most fatigued after doing the exercise. If your chest (pectoralis group) is the sorest or most fatigued after bench pressing, you should do an exercise like the dumbbell fly or a pec deck to strengthen your chest. If your triceps are the sorest or most fatigued, you should do an exercise like triceps extensions to strengthen your triceps.

The fact that movement takes place at only one joint makes single-joint exercises relatively easy to learn; you do not have to learn how to coordinate movement at several joints to do the exercise correctly. This makes single-joint exercises a good choice when you are just starting a program, because you can get on with training without spending a lot of time learning correct exercise technique.

Multi-Joint Exercises

This type of exercise, as the name implies, involves movement at more than one joint and therefore trains more than one muscle group at a time. The characteristics of this type of weight training exercise are essentially the opposite of single-joint exercises. In a multi-joint exercise, the number of repetitions or the amount of weight lifted is limited by the weakest muscle group used in the exercise. Therefore, the muscle group that receives the greatest training stimulus during a multi-joint exercise is the weakest (it must work nearer its maximal ability during the exercise). This means that other muscle groups do not receive an optimal training stimulus during the exercise because they could do more repetitions or lift more weight but are limited by the weakest muscle group.

Multi-joint exercises take more time to learn to do correctly because you must coordinate several muscle groups and even different parts of the muscles involved in the exercise to do the exercises correctly. There is an optimum way to use all the muscles and parts of muscles in a multi-joint exercise to lift the weight. This is why when you are learning to do an exercise, in particular a multi-joint exercise, you make large gains in the amount of weight lifted during the first few weeks of activity.

Multi-joint exercises allow you to have some—although not an optimal—training effect on more muscle groups in a shorter period of time than with single-joint exercises. For example, if you do a leg press, the quadriceps, hamstrings, gluteals, and even the calf muscles are being trained. If you use single-joint exercises to train these same muscle groups, you must do four different exercises, one for each muscle group. So if your training time is limited, it is better to choose multi-joint exercises even though the training stimulus will only be maximal for the weakest muscle group.

Because the weakest muscle group will limit how much weight you can lift or how many repetitions you can do, a good weight training program will use both single-joint and multi-joint exercises. Both have characteristics that make them good exercise choices in certain situations.

Types of Equipment

There are many types of weight training equipment, and more types are being invented and marketed all the time. All types of equipment have characteristics that make them unique. Their uniqueness makes each equipment type a good choice in certain situations.

Body Weight Exercises

Use of your body weight as resistance can be considered a type of weight training. Pull-ups, push-ups, sit-ups, and body weight squats are all body weight exercises. The weight used in this type of exercise is limited to how much the individual weighs. This makes varying the weight used difficult in most situations. It is possible, however, in some body weight exercises to vary the resistance used. For example, you can do a normal push-up with your feet and hands on the floor. You can also do a push-up with your hands on a bench or chair and feet on the floor. In this position, with your hands higher than your feet, the push-up is easier because there is more weight on your feet and so less weight on your hands.

Some people mistakenly believe that body weight exercises are easy to do. This notion is incorrect because for many people, their own body weight is sufficient to cause some strain. Many people cannot do one pull-up.

One characteristic that makes body weight exercises unique is that you always have the equipment (your body) with you to do them. This makes them an excellent choice for on-the-road programs. If a program consists exclusively of body weight exercises, it can be done in a hotel room or in a park. Thus, body weight exercises are an excellent choice for people who travel a lot.

Free Weights

Barbells and dumbbells are free weights. A barbell is a long bar on which weight plates can be placed on both ends. A barbell is normally held with both hands and lifted with two arms, but a dumbbell is normally held with only one hand and lifted with only one arm. There are also other types of bars. One common bar type is an EZ curl bar. This bar is normally lifted with two hands but is not completely straight. It has a handle that is shaped like a *W,* which allows for gripping the bar with the little finger in a position that is lower than the thumb. An EZ curl bar is used in many exercises because the grip allowed relieves stress on the wrist for many individuals.

All of the equipment described above are called free weights because they are not part of a machine and are free to move in all three planes of movement. When lifting free weights they must be balanced or their movement controlled in the up-down, left-right, and forward-backward planes of movement. Because movement must be controlled in all three planes, free weight exercises are relatively difficult to learn to do correctly.

Also, because of the need to control movement in all three planes of movement when lifting a free weight, you have to use muscles not only to lift the weight but also to balance it in all three planes. Therefore, a free weight exercise, compared with a similar machine exercise, requires the use of more muscles or some muscles to a greater extent. For example, executing a free weight bench press requires more muscles than executing a machine bench press because in a machine bench press, you only have to lift the weight and not balance it in the left-right and forward-backward planes of movement.

Some athletic team strength coaches feel that you must balance the weight in all three planes of movement because in daily life and sporting activities, you must also balance your body weight or an external weight, like an opponent, in all three planes. Therefore, the programs for their teams mostly consist of free weight exercises. They still use some machine exercises because it is impossible or dangerous to do some exercises without a machine. For example, it is not safe to do knee extensions or knee curls without a machine.

Weight Training Machines

There are many types of weight training machines, but there are general characteristics that all machines have in common. First, the majority of machines allow movement only in the up-down plane. This means that the muscles which balance the resistance in the other two planes are not heavily involved in the exercise and learning exercise technique is easier than when using free weights. Therefore, machine exercises are a good choice when first starting a weight training program because you can get on with training in a very short period of time and do not need to spend a lot of time learning correct technique.

There are some new machines that do allow movement in two planes, up-down and left-right. These machines require the use of more muscles to balance the resistance in the left-right plane, compared with normal machines. If you have access to these types of machines, use them. They are a good exercise choice, although it will take a little time to learn how to use them correctly.

Most machines also have adjustments such as seat height, so that you can get positioned correctly on the machine. If you cannot get positioned correctly on a machine, you cannot use correct exercise technique. If you cannot use correct technique, you are setting yourself up for an injury. So if you cannot position yourself correctly on a machine, do not use it. In general, machines are built to fit the average adult male, so many women and children may have trouble positioning themselves correctly on some machines.

If a machine will not fit you correctly and you want to do the exercise the machine is made for, you have several choices. First, it may be possible to alter the machine slightly, such as with an added seat pad, to make it fit you. If this is done, make sure the alteration does not make the exercise unsafe in any other way. For example, adding a pad makes the seat height correct, but the pad slides, making the exercise unsafe. Sometimes using the same piece of equipment by a different manufacturer will allow you to adjust the machine to fit you. You can also do a free weight exercise instead, such as doing a dumbbell arm curl instead of a machine arm curl.

All machines have a way to adjust the weight used. On selectorized machines this is done by placing a pin into a weight stack that is built into the machine. On these types of machines it is easy and quick to adjust the weight used. However, you may find that the increments in the weights are quite large. This is especially true if you are just starting out. If you are using 20 pounds to do an exercise and the weight stack increases are 10 pounds, that means when you choose to increase the weight, you must go to 30 pounds. This is a 50 percent increase in the resistance being used and is too large an increase to allow a smooth progression in resistance. In some instances this can be remedied by using small weights that go on top of or attach in some other way to the machine's weight stack.

On plate-loaded machines you place normal weight plates on pegs on the machine to change the weight. This makes it easy to have a small increase in weight because weight plates can weigh as little as 1.25 pounds. However, it takes a little longer to adjust the weight than with selectorized machines.

Some machines use hydraulics or air pressure to supply the resistance. On these machines it is easy to adjust the resistance because it normally involves turning a knob or handle or pushing a button. It is also possible to have small increases in resistance, as it is possible on some of these machines to change the resistance in one-pound increments. This makes it easy to have a smooth progression in the weights used.

Another kind of machine is the variable resistance machine. This type of machine attempts to vary the weight during a repetition by using a

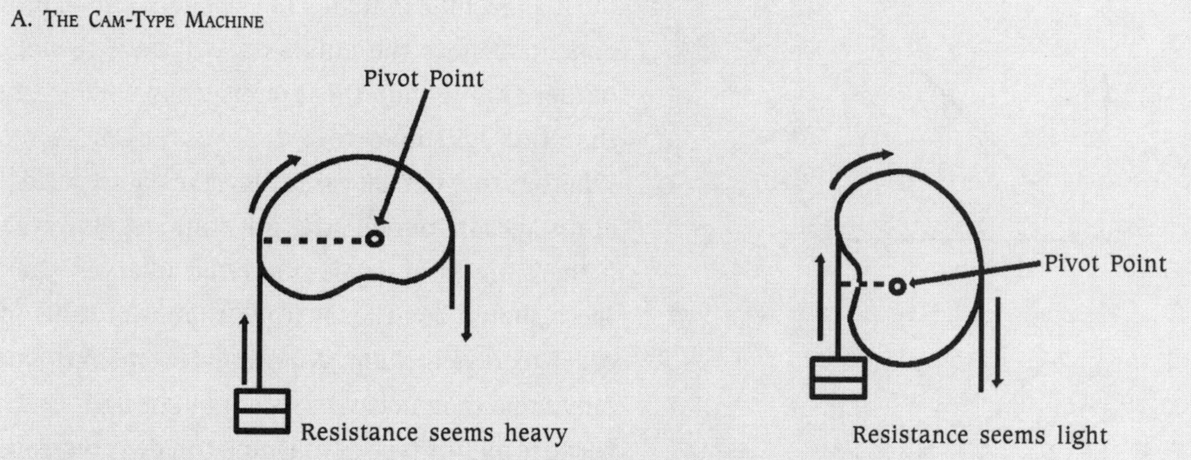

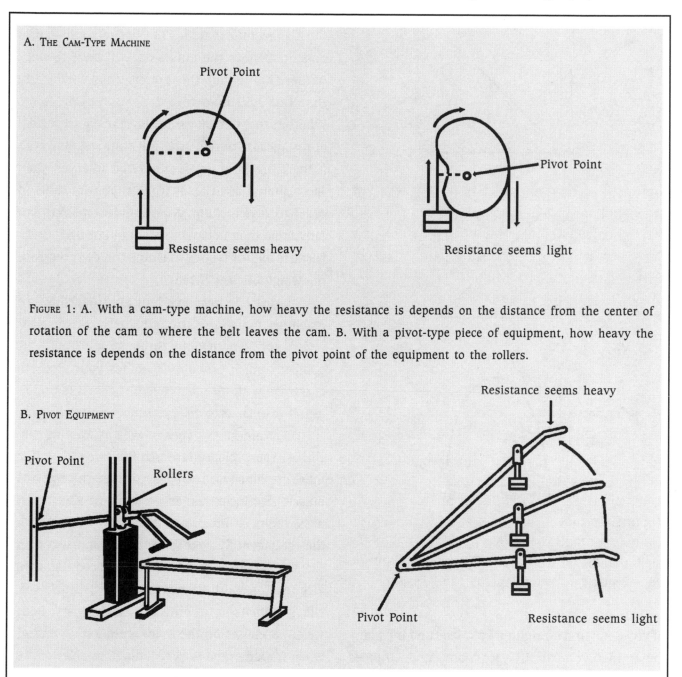

Figure 1: A. With a cam-type machine, how heavy the resistance is depends on the distance from the center of rotation of the cam to where the belt leaves the cam. B. With a pivot-type piece of equipment, how heavy the resistance is depends on the distance from the pivot point of the equipment to the rollers.

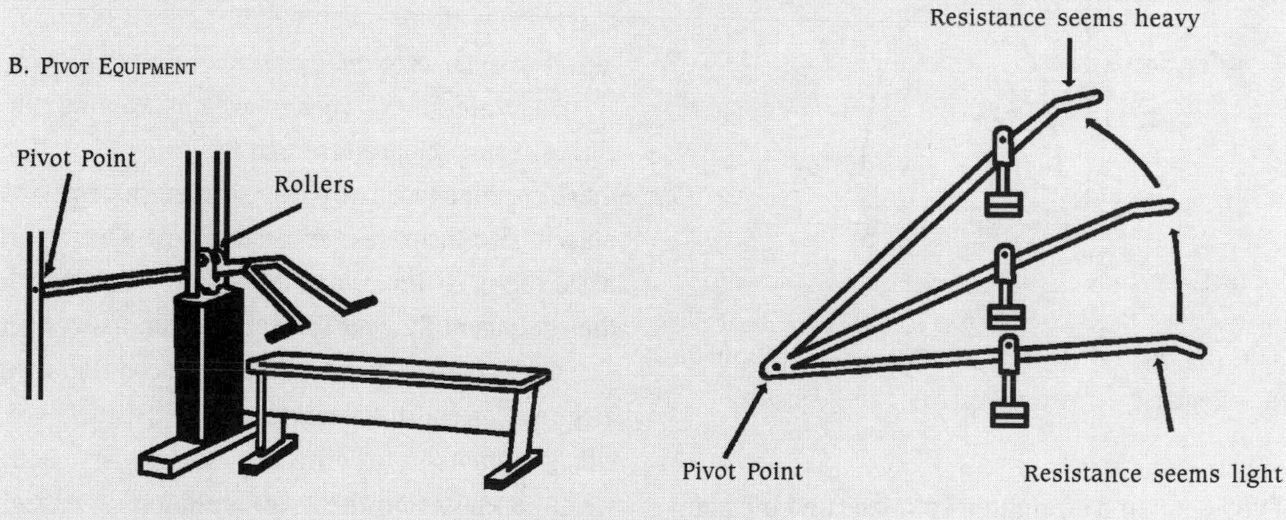

cam or pivot equipment. If the distance from the pivot point of the cam to where the chain or strap leaves the cam is long the weight seems heavy, and if this distance is short the weight seems light (Figure 1). On pivot equipment, the greater the distance the rollers are from the pivot point of the machine, the heavier the resistance seems.

One goal of variable resistance machines is to match the strength curve of the exercise being performed. All exercises have a strength curve, which means you are stronger and weaker at various points in the exercise movement. There are three major types of strength curves (Figure 2).

An ascending strength curve means as you lift the weight from its lowest position it seems to get lighter and lighter. A squat has an ascending strength curve. If you only do a half squat you can lift more than if you do a full squat, and

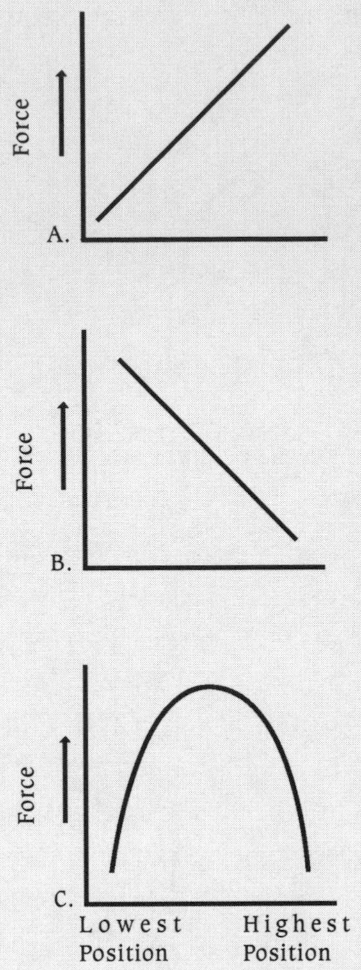

Figure 2: There are three major types of strength curves: A. ascending, B. descending, and C. bell-shaped.

if you bend and straighten your legs and hips only by an inch you can lift a lot more. A bench press also has an ascending strength curve. An upright row has a descending strength curve. The higher you lift the weight from the lowest position, the heavier it seems. If you only lift the weight halfway up you can lift more weight than if you lifted it all the way up. The third type of strength curve is bell shaped. As you lift the weight at first it is easier to lift, and then it becomes harder to lift, then easier again. An arm curl and a knee curl have bell shaped strength curves.

If a machine matches the strength curve, proponents believe the muscle(s) will have to work harder throughout the exercise movement and that this will lead to greater strength gains. Whether this is true or not receives a great deal of discussion among strength trainers. However, if there are three types of strength curves, then there should be at least three shapes of cams in order to match them. A lever-type machine can only hope to match an ascending strength curve because all this type of machine can do is increase the weight as it is lifted.

Sport science research indicates that cam-type machines match the strength curves of some exercises for some people. So if the machine feels good to you, it probably matches your strength curve. As with all machines, proper fit is important if you expect to use proper exercise technique.

There are many types of weight training machines. Sport science research indicates that all of these machine types can lead to strength gains and muscle size increases. So in terms of general fitness, the most important issue is whether or not the equipment fits you so that you can use correct exercise technique. Another important consideration is the equipment characteristics that will benefit specific situations in training. For example, use body weight exercises on the road, multi-joint exercises when training time is very limited, or selectorized equipment when training time is limited.

Accessory Equipment

As in other sports or activities, there are several pieces of accessory equipment that can be used when weight training. Items like gloves, belts, and special shoes can be used if desired but are not a necessity for safe and effective weight training. Accessory equipment may be used because it has certain characteristics that some people like or use to meet the goals of their weight training program.

Lifting Shoes

Virtually every sport or activity has shoes that are specifically designed for it, and weight training is no different. Weight training shoes are designed with a hard sole and heel so that any force developed by the legs and hips is used to lift the weight and not to compress the sole or heel of the shoe. This type of shoe construction enables one to lift a little more weight. Running shoes are designed to cushion the force of the foot hitting the ground while running or jogging, which can be up to two to three times body weight with every foot strike. So these two types of shoes are built to do totally different things.

Another reason for the hard sole and heel in a weight lifting shoe is balance. If you are doing an exercise like a squat with a heavy weight and you get the weight on your shoulders and then your heel sinks a little because the heel is soft, you could lose your balance. This is also why it is not a good idea to lift weights in running shoes.

If you are not a competitive weight lifter, it is not necessary to invest in an expensive pair of weight lifting shoes. However, it is not recommended that you lift in running shoes. A pair of cross-trainers will meet the needs of most fitness or recreational weight trainers.

Belts and Breathing

Weight training belts are wide in the back and designed to support the lower back during lifting. These belts do support the lower back, but not in the way that most people think they do. The belts do not support the back by keeping the bones of the spinal column, or vertebrae, from sliding backward. If a belt was needed for this, you would not be lifting; in fact, you probably would be paralyzed.

When lifting a heavy weight, one tends to hold one's breath in what is termed a Valsalva maneuver. This involves holding the breath and then trying to exhale against a closed glottis. The result is an increase in intrathoracic and intra-abdominal pressure, which helps to keep the lower back—in fact, the entire back—upright. The pressure pushes against the vertebrae from the front and supports them from the front. It also helps to keep your rib cage upright, which helps to support the upper back and keep you from bending over at the lower back. A belt helps to increase intra-abdominal pressure because it does not allow the abdominal muscles to bulge forward and so allows the buildup of more pressure.

Think of your abdominal cavity as a balloon. If the balloon cannot get any bigger yet more air is forced into it, the pressure inside the balloon rises. The belt keeps the abdominal cavity from getting any bigger so when you hold your breath, more pressure builds up and helps support the back.

In reality a belt is a crutch for weak abdominals. Strengthening the abdominals will allow the build up of more intra-abdominal pressure to support the lower back without a belt. If you are going to do exercises with a lot of weight and your lower back needs support, then a belt can help you. However, a better long-term strategy is to strengthen your abdominals and lower back muscles so that you can support the weight and keep your lower back straight without a belt.

If you are going to use a belt, do not keep it cinched tightly except during the sets of exercises where lower back support is needed. Wearing a belt that is cinched tightly even when not lifting increases your blood pressure. This is true even during an activity like riding a stationary bike. If you have a history of cardiovascular problems, do not wear a belt or excessively hold your breath during lifting. Both will increase your blood pressure, which makes the heart's work of pumping blood more difficult.

You should breathe during each and every repetition you do. This normally is done by inhaling as you lower the weight and exhaling as you lift the weight. Toward the end of a difficult set you will tend to hold your breath. This is not necessarily bad, but this is when you must try to remember to breathe during each repetition.

Gloves

Weight training gloves are normally fingerless. Thus they protect the palms from the knurls on many barbells, dumbbells, and weight equipment handles yet allow a good "feel" of the bar. They also help prevent blisters and calluses from developing on the palm area. Gloves are not, however, necessary for a safe and effective weight training program.

Make informed decisions about types of equipment and accessories that you will use in your program.

Chapter *Four*

Weight Room Safety

Overall, weight training is a very safe activity. In fact, there is less chance of an injury during weight training than when playing basketball or squash. The most common injuries during weight training are sprains and strains. Things that can and should be done in order to decrease the chance of injury include using spotters, maintaining equipment, and the application of common sense.

Physical Examination

Before starting any exercise program, including weight training, you should get a complete physical. Ideally the examination should be performed by a physician who understands sports medicine. A complete physical examination is especially important if you are 40 years or older. The examination should be repeated on a yearly basis. Ideally it should include a graded exercise test (GXT). A GXT is a test normally done using a treadmill or stationary bike. During a GXT running or cycling is progressively made more and more difficult while your heart rate and the electrical activity of your heart are monitored (the latter by means of electrocardiography, or EKG). If any abnormal response to the exercise is found, the test may be stopped. The information obtained during the GXT can then be used to help put together your physical training program in a safe manner.

There are some contraindications to exercise and factors that may show up on a physical examination. The following factors should be considered when putting together your weight training program:

1. Abnormal hemodynamic response: for example, an abnormal blood pressure response upon moving from a seated to a standing position (i.e., orthostatic hypertension).
2. Abnormal EKG during the GXT: an abnormal heart rate or other indicator of abnormal heart response to exercise.
3. Impaired left ventricular function: an abnormal response of the heart in terms of pumping blood.
4. Uncontrolled high blood pressure: an inability

to control high blood pressure with normal medications.

5. Cardiac arrhythmia: an abnormal resting heart rate response to exercise.
6. Low exercise ability: exercise ability that is not greater than six times your resting caloric use (i.e., 6 METS, or metabolic equivalents).
7. Orthopedic problems: knee or back problems, arthritis, or less than normal range of motion at a joint.

In general, your weight training can be altered to account for most physical problems. It is better to know about a physical problem and alter your workout than to not know about a problem and injure yourself. So get a physical examination before starting your weight training program, and use the information in consultation with your physician to design a program that will ensure long-term success.

Spotters

A spotter is someone who will help the lifter if needed. In general, spotting is needed more when using free weights than when using weight training machines or body weight exercises. This is mainly due to the fact that free weights can potentially fall on the lifter or someone else if control of them is lost. The general rules of spotting are as follows:

The spotter or spotters must be strong enough to lift the weight by themselves if really needed. The classic example of breaking this rule is a 90-pound weakling spotting a 250-pounder pressing 300 pounds. The spotter is not strong enough to completely lift the weight if needed for the safety of the lifter. All that this spotter may be able to do is call for help.

Some exercises require two spotters to be spotted safely. This is especially true for some dumbbell exercises and barbell exercises where heavy weights are used. For example, when doing an exercise like the dumbbell bench press, it is almost impossible for one spotter to quickly assist both arms of the lifter or take the dumbbells completely from the lifter if needed. The same is true for some barbell exercises like the back squat or bench press.

Spotting Rules

√ Spotter(s) must be strong enough to assist lifter

√ Use of two spotters may be necessary to ensure safety in lifts

√ Spotters need to know how many repetitions are to be attempted

√ Spotters must be attentive to the lifter at all times

√ Spotter should stop the set if exercise technique deteriorates

√ Free weight exercises require spotters more so than do machine exercises

Spotting is not a difficult task, but it needs to be done attentively to ensure the lifter's safety. Following the rules given in Table 1 will ensure safe and effective spotting. Remember, you only really need to be in need of a spotter once to be injured.

Weight Room Etiquette

Another aspect of weight room safety is weight room etiquette. Everyone has experienced impolite actions in the weight room that do not make for a safe weight training environment. Horseplay of all types should not be tolerated. It can distract a lifter and result in an injury.

All lifters should be given sufficient room to perform an exercise. This means that there needs to be enough room between pieces of equipment for their safe use. It also means that lifters must respect one another's space. For example, do not take a weight plate off of a weight rack that is right next to someone who is in the middle of a set or walk right in front of a lifter during the middle of a set. Most people are trying to get their workout done in as short a period of time as possible, but being impolite to other lifters in order to save time can result in injury. Do not put yourself or another lifter in danger of an injury by being impolite in the weight room.

Equipment Safety

It is foolish to use a piece of equipment you know to be in need of repair, even if it is still available for use. Many clubs place a placard on equipment that needs repair stating something like "Temporarily Out of Use." Obey these placards; they are for your own safety. If you notice something unsafe, like a badly worn cable or strap on a piece of equipment, notify the management of the club immediately and do not use the equipment. Do not put yourself knowingly in danger of an injury.

Equipment Fit

Proper fit was discussed in Chapter 3. Correct exercise technique requires that a weight training machine fits you properly. If the machine cannot be adjusted to fit you properly, correct exercise technique is impossible. If a machine cannot be adjusted to fit you properly, do not use it, as injury could result. In most cases a substitute exercise for a muscle group can be performed—for example, a body weight exercise or an exercise performed on another manufacturer's equipment, with free weights, or with some other type of equipment, like rubber tubing.

Use of Collars

On many pieces of equipment, especially barbells and some types of dumbbells, collars (a device that keeps the weights from sliding off the ends of the bar) are needed for safety. Some dumbbells are one solid piece, the weights are part of the bar or permanently attached to the bar, and in this case collars are not needed. But if the weights are not secured and the bar is slanted to one side the weight plates will slide. This puts you off balance and in danger of injury. The weight plates may also completely slide off the bar and possibly hit you, your spotter, or even a bystander. So use collars on equipment where needed.

Revolving Handles

Many barbells have a revolving collar on each end, and some machines have revolving handles. These moving parts ensure that the handle or bar can turn in your hand when you are lifting, which in turn helps prevent the buildup of calluses and facilitates using the correct technique. Ripping of the skin on your hand may also occur if the handle is supposed to revolve and does not. If a handle or bar is supposed to revolve, it is a good idea to give the bar or handle a spin to make sure it is revolving freely prior to using it.

Breathing

During any physical activity—whether it be weight training, swimming, running, or anything else—your blood pressure will increase during the activity. It will then return to normal after the activity. In fact, physical activity may lower your resting blood pressure over time, especially if you have high blood pressure.

If you hold your breath and try to exhale at the same time, or perform a Valsalva maneuver, your blood pressure will also increase. This is true whether you just sit and hold your breath or do any other physical activity and hold your breath. When your blood pressure increases during physical activity, that increase make it more difficult for your heart to pump blood; if you hold your breath at the same time, the combined increases in blood pressure make your heart work harder.

During weight training, if you hold your breath, your blood pressure will increase at a greater rate than if you did not hold your breath. This is why you are told not to hold your breath while weight training. The recommended pattern of breathing when weight training is to inhale when lowering the weight and exhale when lifting the weight during each and every repetition. You should make sure you are breathing properly to help keep your blood pressure low while weight training.

With that said, it is natural to hold your breath when you are lifting a heavy object such as during weight training. So the key is not to hold your breath excessively. You will tend to hold your breath during the last few repetitions of a set to failure (doing repetitions until you cannot do any more). Do not hold your breath continuously for a complete repetition or several repetitions in a row.

There are other things that will minimize the increase in blood pressure when weight training. Your blood pressure will gradually increase while a set is performed and will reach a maximum during the last repetitions of a set. As stated earlier you will tend to hold your breath during the last repetitions of a set to failure, which will increase your blood pressure even more. So if you are trying to minimize the increase in blood pressure, do not carry sets to complete failure.

The increase in blood pressure will also increase proportionately the more muscle mass used during the exercise. Thus higher pressure will occur during an exercise like squats or leg presses, where a lot of muscle mass is used, compared with exercises like knee extensions or knee curls, which require the use of a smaller amount of muscle mass. So if you are trying to limit the increase in blood pressure, you may not want to do large muscle mass exercises like squats, leg presses, or bench presses. This is especially true when you first start weight training. If you have high resting blood pressure or any other cardiovascular problem, you should consult with your physician and use all of the above information to minimize the increase in blood pressure when weight training.

Weight training is a very safe physical activity. Most aspects of weight training safety are related to proper exercise technique, spotting, or the proper functioning of equipment. Making sure you understand all these aspects will make a safe activity even safer.

Chapter *Five*

Exercise Variety: The Spice of Weight Training

Many people do the same weight training routine for months or even years, complaining daily that they are making no fitness gains. And all of us have heard comments like, "I do not want to weight train because I do not want to get any bigger, but I do want to be stronger," or "My program is just not producing the gains I want." All weight training will result in some gains in strength, muscle size, and local muscular endurance. However, some combinations of exercise patterns and repetitions will result in greater gains in strength or muscle size than others. Not all weight training sessions are created equal in terms of specific fitness gains. A major reason to understand training variation is so that you can put your program together in a way that results in the types of fitness gains you want.

Why Vary Training?

Everyone has heard that they need to vary their training, but few people actually vary it enough to create optimal fitness gains. There are some very compelling reasons to vary your weight training or any type of physical training for that matter.

One reason many people believe in varying training is to keep from becoming bored. If you are just going through the motions of weight training exercises and not pushing yourself a little, you cannot expect much of a gain in anything.

Did you ever notice that when you start doing a new exercise, for a couple of weeks you make some large gains in strength quickly? One reason for this is, the new exercise is a new stimulus for adaptations that result in increased strength. If you stay with the same training program too long, it is no longer a new stimulus for your body to make adaptations resulting in fitness gains.

If you stay with the same program for several months, you will plateau—make no gains in fitness even though you are training hard. Most people say to themselves, "I must not be working hard enough!" when they reach a leveling-off point in their development. They work even harder but still remain on the plateau and do not make fitness gains. What they need to do to get off of the plateau is make a change in their training, not neccessarily work harder. This may mean doing more or fewer repetitions per set or changing the exercises being performed.

Things That Can Be Changed

Virtually anything that can be changed in a weight training session can be varied to bring about desired changes in your body. The key is to make changes that bring about the desired results in strength, muscle size, or local muscular endurance and not those that are unwanted. For example, a women goes to a health club and says to the trainer, "I want to lift weights because I want to get stronger, but I do not want my muscles to get any bigger and I do not have a lot of time." At many health clubs she will be given a standard workout prescription of eight to ten exercises, ten repetitions per set and three sets of each exercise. In addition, she will be told to perform each set to failure and because she does not have a lot of time, to use one-minute rest periods between sets and exercises.

What is wrong with this workout for this woman's training goals? You will discover in this chapter that this workout will make her stronger, but it will make her muscles bigger also! This workout is a prescription to increase muscle size, exactly what she said she did not want. There are differences between different weight training sessions. Knowing what to change and how to change it will help you put together a weight training session that brings about only the changes you want.

Things That Can Be Changed

- √ Number of repetitions
- √ Weight used
- √ Number of sets
- √ Exercise choice
- √ Number of exercises
- √ Exercise order
- √ Rest periods

Number of Repetitions

The number of repetitions (reps) per set is easily varied to bring about desired changes in fitness. A rep is one complete movement of an exercise and normally consists of lifting the weight and then lowering the weight. Virtually any number of reps per set from 1 to 20 will bring about some increase in strength, muscle size, and local muscular endurance. Strength is the ability to lift a heavy weight for a small number of reps, and local muscular endurance is the ability to do a moderate number of reps with a medium or light weight. However, different numbers of reps will emphasize to a greater extent an increase in strength, muscle size, or local muscular endurance. In general, small numbers of reps emphasize strength; medium numbers of reps, muscle size; and large numbers of reps, local muscular endurance.

This is not to say that doing 20 reps does not result in some strength gain. However, the strength gain will be less than if you did 6 reps per set. In addition, this does not mean that doing 6 reps will only bring about an increase in strength and that doing 7 reps will bring about only an increase in muscle size. The number of reps per set is a continuum—as the number increases there is a gradual switch from strength, to muscle size, and then to local muscular endurance gains. It is not an all-or-nothing proposition. The number of reps per set, like all things that can be varied, should be chosen and varied to meet the goals of the lifter.

Repetition Continuum

Reps	Goal
3–6 reps	Strength
7–12 reps	Muscle size
10–20 reps	Local muscular endurace

Most programs will prescribe a range of reps per set, such as 5 to 6 or 10 to 12. When the lifter can do the upper limit of the range, then the exercise is made more difficult by adding more weight. Because more weight is used, the lifter will drop back down to the lower limit of the rep range. As the lifter again makes strength gains and once again can do the upper limit of the range with the heavier weight, the weight is once again increased.

Intensity

Closely linked to the number of reps is the intensity, or weight used. It is impossible to do a lot of reps with a heavy weight. However, it is possible to do only a couple of reps with a light weight even if you could do more. Because of this a lot of people waste a lot of training time and wonder why they are not making any fitness gains. For example, your goal is to increase your strength, so you choose to do 5 to 6 reps per set, but you choose to use a weight that you really could do 10 reps with. This will result in little or no gain in strength, muscle size, or local muscular endurance because it is too easy to do. For any change in your body to take place, you must ask your body to do more or at least close to more than it presently can do. In terms of weight training, it means the last few reps in a set do not have to be impossible, but they must be difficult to complete if you expect to make a gain in any fitness variable. The same is true for any type of physical training. If you want to increase your flexibility, you have to do some stretching. You do not have to stretch to the point where the pain is unbearable, but you do need to feel that the muscle is being stretched if you expect to achieve an increase in flexibility.

Because of the need for the last few reps in a set to be difficult, many programs use what is called a repetition maximum, or RM, as discussed in Chapter 2. An RM allows the performance of x reps per set, but not x+1 reps per set. The use of an RM weight for a certain range in number of reps (e.g., 5 to 6 for strength) ensures that you will be training hard enough to bring about the gains in fitness you want. Again, this does not mean that each and every set must be performed using an RM weight, but that somewhere in your training program, at least on a weekly basis, each exercise is performed with close to an RM weight.

The easiest way to find an RM for a certain exercise is by a little trial and error. Let's say you want to do 8 reps of an exercise at an 8 RM. It is always best to underestimate your abilities a little at first. This will help in avoiding excessive soreness and in preventing injuries because you are using too heavy a weight for the number of reps you want to do. So initially choose a weight that will allow you to easily do the number of reps you want to do, in this case 8. If it is easy to do the 8 reps for the number of sets you are doing, at the next training session increase the weight slightly. If you cannot do 8 reps, decrease the weight slightly at the next training session. In a couple of sessions you will have safely found your 8 RM for that exercise.

As explained above, the number of reps done and the fitness gains in strength, muscle size, or local muscular endurance are a continuum. So if you are trying to maximize your strength, your program might call for three sets of 4 to 6 reps per set. If you use a true 6 RM weight at the beginning, you will probably wind up doing something like 6, 5, and 4 reps in the first, second, and third sets, respectively. This is all right as you are still in the strength zone of the repetition continuum. The exact number of reps performed is not the only important thing. What is important is that you are in the correct zone of the repetition continuum so that you get the type of fitness gain you desire.

You will not want to be using a true RM weight when you are learning a new exercise. When learning a new exercise you want to be able to do at least 10 reps easily. This will allow you to concentrate on how to do the exercise and not on simply trying to move the weight at all costs. After you have mastered the new exercise over a week or two of training, you can proceed to finding your RM weight.

Let's say you have been weight training for over a year and are now as strong or as big as you desire to be. However, you still want to weight train because you know that as soon as you quit training, you will start to lose strength and muscle size. What can you do? One thing you can do is use slightly less than your true RM weight for the number of reps you are doing. For example, your true 10 RM is 100 pounds. You choose to use 95 pounds and do only 10 reps even though you could do more. Because you are strong enough to do more than 10 reps, your body is not being asked to work hard and you will not make any more large gains in strength or muscle size. In this example it is important to note that you choose not to work at an RM and so choose not to make any more gains in fitness. This did not just happen because you did not understand what you were doing.

Number of Sets

The minimal number of sets of any exercise you can do is one. One set will cause an increase in strength, muscle size, and local muscular endurance. This is especially true when you are just beginning a weight training program, because any training will be more than you have been doing. In addition, because one set is not a high volume of training (i.e., high total number of reps), a one-set program will not make you excessively sore. So one set of each exercise is a good way to start a weight training program. Then after you have become accustomed to doing some weight training, you can choose, if you desire, to increase the number of sets you are doing.

After you have been training a while, one set of an exercise will continue to bring about increases in fitness. The gains over the long haul, however, will not be as great as with a multiple-set program. So as you get in better and better shape, it may require more sets at some point in your program to continue to make fitness gains. At the same time, as with most things, you can also overdo the number of sets. In general, for recreational lifting or general fitness lifting, three sets of an exercise is the maximal number most people will do.

In reality, the three-set guideline applies to training each muscle group. It is possible to be doing a one-set program and still be training a muscle group with more than one set. You could do three different exercises for the same muscle group. For example, you could do machine, hammer, and EZ curl bar arm curls, all for one set, in the same workout. All of these exercises train the biceps muscle group found on the front of your upper arm. This could be called a one-set program, but you are doing a total of three sets for the biceps muscle group. So you have to look at not only at how many sets of each exercise are being performed but how many sets are being performed by a particular muscle group to get an idea of the training volume being done by a muscle group in a training session.

Exercise Choice and Number of Exercises

When you decide what exercises to do, you decide what muscle groups you are going to train. If you see a weight training program that includes three different exercises for the triceps, the muscle on the back of your upper arm, all for three sets, it is apparent that an increase in triceps strength, size, or local muscular endurance is important to the person doing that program.

For a general fitness program, at least one exercise for each major muscle group should be performed. This means that if a total body training session (a session in which all major muscle groups are trained) is performed, 10 to 12 exercises will be done. If improving a certain muscle group is important to you, it is possible to choose to do more than one exercise for that muscle group in a training session. As a general rule, three exercises for a muscle group will be all the training that a particular muscle group can take. If you do decide to start doing more than one exercise for a muscle group, give that muscle group time to adapt to the increased amount of work performed, or volume of training. For example, you are doing one exercise for the back of your upper arm, or triceps. If you add another exercise for the triceps, start off by doing only one set of the new exercise for at least one week. Then add one set every week until you get to the desired number of sets. This will help you avoid excessive soreness and fatigue.

Each exercise for a muscle group trains different portions of a muscle to varying degrees; that is, each exercise emphasizes slightly different areas of a muscle. This is one reason body builders do several different exercises for a certain muscle group. They know each exercise trains different areas of a muscle to varying degrees, and they want to develop the entire muscle.

For general fitness it is a good idea to change the exercise you are doing for a certain muscle group every month or couple of months. This will help your program stay interesting and help to develop the muscle to its fullest potential. For example, you could be doing machine triceps extensions and switch to triceps push-downs using a high pulley for a month and then go back to doing machine triceps extensions or a completely different triceps exercise.

Exercise Order

Exercise order does impact how stressful the training session is. There are many possible ways to arrange the exercise order in a training session. However, all exercise orders involve variations of alternating muscle groups or performing exercises for the same muscle group or body part in succession. An example of alternating muscle groups is performing the bench press, leg press, and lat pull-down, in that order. In this case the exercises are alternated between the upper and lower body. The leg press acts like a partial rest period between the upper body exercises and so makes the training seem less stressful to the upper body because more recovery time is allowed between the upper body exercises. This same thing can be done by alternating exercises between any number of muscle groups. For example, another alternating order is arm curl, knee extension, triceps push-down, and knee curl. Alternating exercises is a good order to use when just starting to do weight training because it is a less stressful order than a non-alternating order.

Stacking, or performing exercises for the same muscle group or body part in succession is the opposite of an alternating order. An example of stacking would be doing the bench press, military press, and triceps push-down. In all three exercises, the triceps is being used. This makes the training seem more stressful to the triceps than when using an alternating order. Stacking can be considered an advanced order because it is more stressful for a muscle group. Stacking is used by many bodybuilders in an attempt to bring about muscle size gains.

For a good progression of exercise stress, stacking of exercises should be preceded by doing the exercises in an alternating order. When you first switch from an alternating to a stacking order, the weight you can use for a certain number of reps will be less because stacking is more stressful. If you decide to make a training session more stressful by using a stacking order, it is a good idea to gradually accustom yourself to the new order. This can be done by using a stacking order for only one session a week and using an alternating order during the rest of the week's sessions for a couple of weeks. Then add another stacked order session every one or two weeks until you are using a stacked order in as many sessions as you desire.

Another way to arrange your exercises is by using a priority order. This means that you will do the exercises that are most important to your goals early in the session before you are fatigued. It will be possible to use slightly more weight for the exercises that are done before fatigue starts to set in. This is one way to place emphasis on exercises and muscle groups with which you want to achieve fitness gains. Let's say you want to emphasize your legs. Having a priority order means that you will do the leg exercises early in your training sessions. This allows you to really attack the leg exercises before you start to fatigue. Use of a priority order does mean you will probably have to do some stacking of exercises. So remember to gradually accustom yourself to using a priority order in a fashion similar to accustoming yourself to a stacking exercise order.

Rest Periods Between Sets

Rest periods between sets and exercises determine how much recovery is allowed before going on to the next set or exercise. This has an impact on how stressful the session is and how much resistance can be used for the desired number of repetitions in the next set. In addition, how long the rest period is has a major influence on the training adaptations that will take place. For example, if short rest periods of 30 seconds are used, little recovery between sets will occur. This means that a true RM weight for a desired number of reps for several sets in a row will be impossible to use because of fatigue. If a training goal of a session is to develop maximal strength, short rest periods will not be used, because one aspect of developing strength is the need to use heavy resistance. This means that long rest periods must be used so that enough recovery takes place and thus heavy resistance can be used.

The length of the rest period between sets and exercises should be chosen to match the goals of the training session. In general, short rest periods are used when the goal is increased cardiovascular fitness. So short rest periods are used when doing circuit weight training. This type of training involves doing 10 to 15 reps per set with 30 second rest periods. With this type of training, the heart rate is kept relatively high, an indication that cardiovascular fitness gains will

Rest Period Guidelines

Length	Duration	Goal
Short	30 seconds	Increase cardiovascular endurance
Medium	1 minute	Increase muscle size
Long	2 minutes or longer	Increase maximal strength

take place. However, remember that weight training is not a good training tool to bring about gains in cardiovascular fitness. Traditional aerobic training will cause about three to five times the gain in cardiovascular fitness as circuit weight training. If a major goal of your training is to gain cardiovascular fitness, some aerobic, or endurance, training must be included in your total training program.

Medium-length rest periods of one minute or so are used when the desire is to increase muscle size. Medium-length rest periods result in a blood hormonal response that over time stimulates an increase in muscle size. Medium-length rest periods also allow enough recovery so that enough weight can be used to stimulate an increase in muscle strength.

Long rest periods allow recovery between sets and thereby permit the use of heavy resistance. They are used when the goal is to emphasize gains in maximal strength. Similar to the number of reps used per set, the rest period length is a continuum. All rest period lengths stimulate an increase in strength, muscle size, and local muscular endurance. However, rest period length also partly determines which of these aspects is emphasized most.

The choices you make when designing a weight training session affect what changes take place in your body. The next chapter discusses how all these choices work together to bring about the desired changes in your body.

Chapter *Six*

All Training Session Variables Work Together

All of the training factors discussed in the last chapter work together to bring about a particular training goal. For example, let's say you decide an increase in arm muscle size is important to you. So you design a training session that has multiple sets of each exercise for the arms and multiple exercises for the biceps and triceps. You also decide to use one-minute rest periods between sets and exercises for your arms so that a hormonal response to bring about increased muscle size takes place. These are all the right decisions, but then you decide to do only 3 reps per set. This is an incorrect training decision because this number of repetitions will emphasize maximal strength and not muscle size increases. The correct decision would be to do about 10 reps per set. When planning your training make sure all your decisions are consistent with your training goals.

All of the exercise training session variables operate on a continuum. So it is possible to design a session for muscle size increases following the guidelines but choosing to do only 6 to 8 reps per set. This means muscle size is being de-emphasized a little at the expense of emphasizing

Guidelines for Training Session Design

Endurance and Tone

short rest periods—30 seconds

10–20 reps per set

exercises for all major muscle groups

work toward stacking exercises for muscle groups

Definition and Muscle Size

medium rest periods—1 minute

7–12 reps per set

exercises for muscle groups in which an increase in size is desired

work toward stacking exercises for muscle groups

Strength

long rest periods—2 minutes or longer

3–6 reps per set

normally 3–6 reps only for multiple joint exercises

initially alternating exercise order

strength a little more. So a session can be designed with any mix of the training session variables you desire. Just keep in mind what is being emphasized and de-emphasized by the total mix of variables in the session.

It is also possible to do one type of program for a certain part of your body and another type for a different part of your body. For example, you may be a runner and desire to increase muscle size in your upper body, but not in your lower body. In this case you would do the exercises for your upper body following a muscle size program, but the exercises for your lower body would be performed following a muscle strength or endurance program, depending upon your individual goals. You could also do a program for endurance and tone for the upper body and definition and muscle size for the lower body if that meets your goals. The possible ways to vary a training session are virtually limitless for meeting your individual needs and goals.

Rest Between Sessions

Changes in the body that result in increased strength, endurance, and muscle size take place during the rest between sessions. These changes do not take place during the session itself. So rest between sessions is very important.

For a total body fitness weight training program, two to three sessions per week should be performed, ideally with 24 to 48 hours between sessions. This does not mean that you cannot perform two sessions on consecutive days in the week if that is all your schedule permits. You will still make fitness gains doing this. It will just seem a little more difficult, especially near the end of that second session, and you will then have to allow more recovery time before doing the next session.

In reality the two to three sessions per week guideline applies to individual muscle groups.

Body-Part Program

Day 1: back, biceps, abdominals

Day 2: front of thighs, calves

Day 3: chest, triceps

Day 4: hamstrings, shoulders

Day 5: no weight training

Day 6: begin again with day 1

So if your sessions are "total body" in nature (have at least one exercise for all major muscle groups), you need only two to three sessions per week. However, you could do four sessions per week and still follow this guideline. In this instance you could do two sessions per week for the lower body, one on Monday and one on Thursday, and two per week for the upper body, one on Tuesday and one on Friday. There are a lot of other possible ways to train each major muscle group following the two to three sessions per week guideline.

Body-part workouts are very popular among bodybuilders, where the major training goal is increased muscle size. In this type of program, each body-part or muscle group is trained only once or twice a week. These types of programs allow for a very high volume of training (multiple exercises for a muscle group and multiple sets of each exercise), with the entire session dedicated to one or two body parts or muscle groups. After such a session it will probably take longer than 24 to 48 hours for the muscle group to recover, but an allowance for recovery is made in this type of program. A body-part program is worth trying if you have a major training goal of increased muscle size and almost daily weight training sessions fit into your schedule.

Two Sessions per Day

The performance of two weight training sessions on the same day is effective for gains and is done by some athletes. Having two sessions on the same day does allow for a greater volume of training. It also allows for the use of more intensity, or heavier resistance, for the same number of repetitions because some recovery will take place between the two sessions on the same day. This is why two sessions on the same day are effective in bringing about gains. But as with body-part programs, you must have the time needed to go to the weight room two times during one day to do such a program. Two sessions per day, however, are not needed to meet the goals of a fitness weight trainer.

Long-Term Training

Obviously, for a long-term program to be effective, it must be performed over the long haul. Several things can help keep someone interested in continuing to do weight training. Not becoming bored with the training and continuing to make fitness gains are very important factors in helping to stay motivated to weight train. Closely tied to continued fitness gains is avoiding training plateaus. Training variation can help with all of these factors.

For general fitness your training should be varied about once every four to eight weeks. This does not mean that you need to change everything about your program. You can vary your training by simply changing one of the things in a training session. You could change some of the exercises for a muscle group. For example, if you are doing a free weight bench press, change to a machine bench press or a dumbbell bench press for a while. If you are doing 12 reps per set, go to 8 per set. If you are doing three sets, go to two sets. If you are using an alternating exercise order go to a stacking order. The change does not mean that everything in your program changes at once.

The change can also be more dramatic. For example, if you do not want to increase your muscle size and are doing an endurance program following the guidelines given above, you could switch to a program emphasizing strength following the guidelines given above. There are many possible variations in weight training, and you should vary your training to help ensure long-term gains. Just keep in mind how the change in the program will affect the desired changes in your body.

Chapter *Seven*

Tracking Your Gains

How large your gains in muscle size, muscle strength, or any other fitness parameter over the long haul are is dependent on two major characteristics that you can control. The first is how good of shape you are in. The second is how good the program you are doing is. Your genetics have a major impact on how large your fitness gains will be—but that is something you cannot control.

During the first few weeks or even months of weight training, you will make rapid gains. This is due in large part to the fact that you probably are in relatively poor condition. Therefore, the potential to improve is very great. The second reason you will make large gains at the beginning of a program is that you are "learning" to do the exercises in your weight training program. The majority of this "learning" happens during the first several weeks of a program and results in large gains in strength.

Some changes in the "quality" of muscle protein that start to take place during the first several weeks of training. These changes in quality can result in increased strength but have no impact on muscle size.

If you have weight trained before but are just starting again after a period of doing no weight training, you will also experience a large increase in strength due to "relearning" how to do the exercises. However, the gain in strength will not be as large as for someone who never weight trained before.

After the initial large gain in strength, increases will slow down because further gains are dependent in large part on increases in the amount of protein making up the muscle. Increasing the protein in a muscle is a slower process than "learning" to do the exercise, so gains also slow down. There may also be continued changes in the quality of protein making up the muscle, which could also contribute to further strength gains.

An understanding of the above factors is important when establishing realistic goals for strength, muscle size, or any other fitness factor related to weight training. When you are just starting a program, a goal of increasing your bench press weight by 100 percent may be realistic and attainable. However, if you have been weight training for a year, this same goal is probably unrealistic and unattainable. A more realistic goal may be to increase your bench press weight by 15 to 25 percent in this instance. If you are a very well trained athlete, a realistic goal may be only a 2 to 3 percent increase in your bench press weight over a year of training. This same concept of decreasing gains the better shape you are in applies to all fitness variables, from muscle size to cardiovascular endurance.

Tracking Your Program

Now that you have an understanding of the magnitude of gains to expect at different times in a training program, let's discuss some reasons to track your training. Did you ever see someone with a puzzled look on their face standing next to a piece of equipment as if saying to themselves, "Now what weight did I use last time?" One reason to track the progress of your program is to simply know what weights you are using for different exercises. The most common reasons to track or keep a training log of your program are as follows:

- to know what has been done in previous sessions
- to note progress as the program progresses
- to have a record of a program that did not work for you so that you do not repeat it
- to have a record of a program that did work for you so that you can repeat it
- to make changes in a program that did work for you to make it even better
- to know when it is time to make a change in the program

All of these reasons to keep track of your program will ensure long-term enjoyment of and long-term success with your weight training program. Now that we know why we should track the progress of a weight training program, we need to discuss how to track a program or keep a training log. A training log is nothing more than a written record of what was done. There are three major types of training logs. The first is a computer record of what was done. Some types of weight training equipment are connected to a computer that automatically compiles what is done as it is being done. This type of training log is available on only a couple of manufacturers' equipment. It may be the wave of the future, but for now it is available only to those of us who train in a weight room that has such equipment. So most of us have to keep track of things the old-fashioned way—by writing them down.

There are two major ways of keeping a written training log. One way involves using a printed card and the other using a notebook in which to record what was done. Many clubs and spas use a printed card on which to keep a training log. There are as many versions of a printed card as there are clubs and spas. However, they are all essentially the same. There are places for your name, dates of workouts, exercises, weight used, and sets and repetitions performed. Some will also have a place to record body weight and a place for comments about the training program. On some printed cards the exercises of a standard workout will be printed in the exercise column. On others the exercise column will be blank and the lifter or an instructor fills in the exercises. An example of a printed workout card is shown in Figure 1.

Most workout cards are set up for a total-body workout. If you are going to do any other type of workout, the second version of a training log, us-

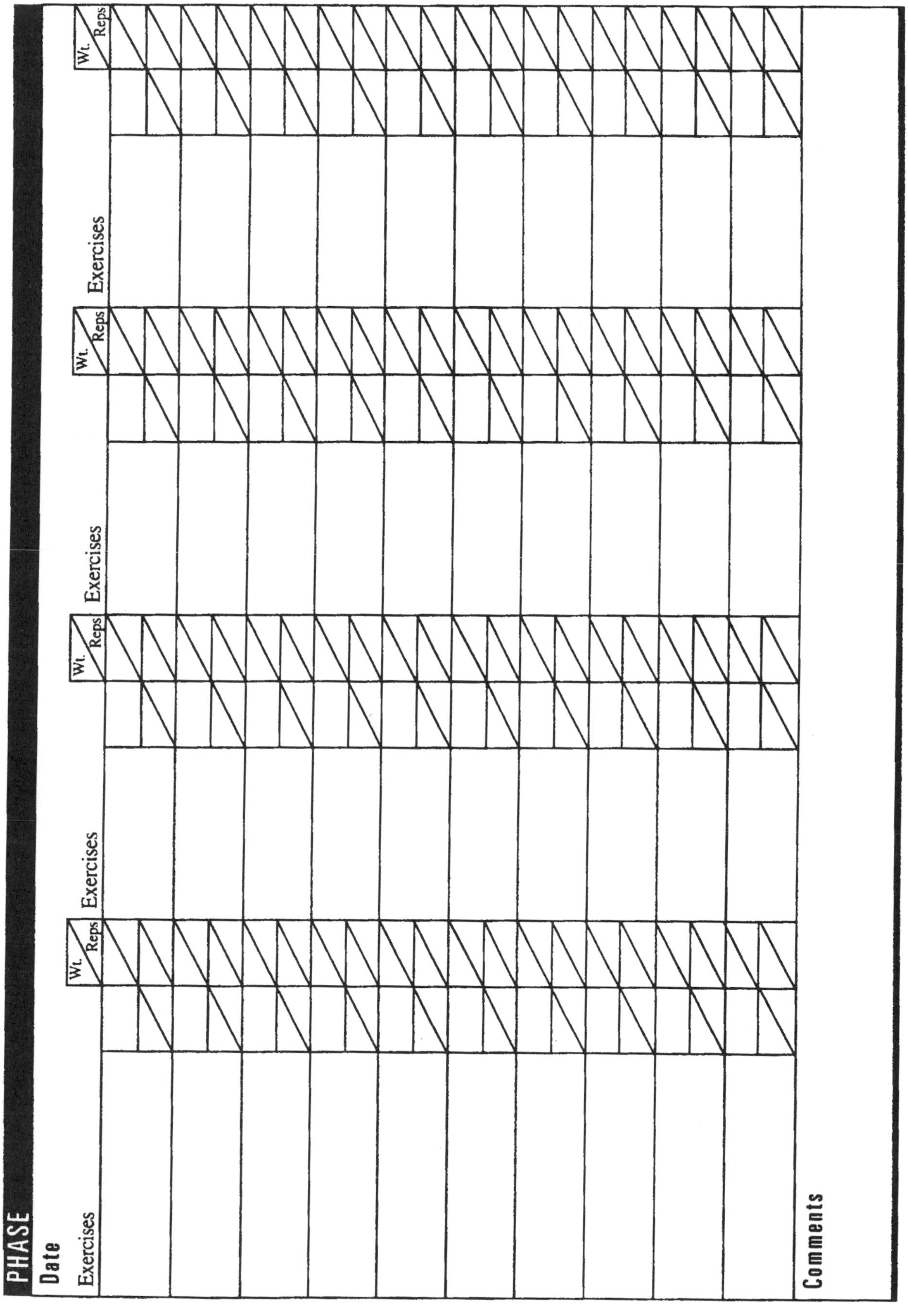

Figure 1: Example of printed workout card

ing a notebook in which to record the training sessions and other pertinent information, may work better for you. In order to record the workout quickly, many lifters use a type of shorthand. For example, the notation "leg press 2 x 8 @ 200" means two sets each of 8 reps using 200 pounds for the leg press. Another example, "chest press 3 x 6, 5, 5 @ 150, 150, 160" means the chest press is to be performed for three sets with the first set consisting of 6 reps and the other two sets 5 reps. The first two sets are to be done using 150 pounds, and the last set is to be done with 160 pounds. How you abbreviate when recording your workout is not important as long as you understand what the training log means.

It is important that you record not only what was planned to be done but also what was actually done during the workout. This information is important in planning the coming workouts. What was planned is presented in the left part of the notation in Figure 2. What was actually done is noted after the abbreviation "act," meaning actual. For example, 3 x 8 @ 130 for the lat pull-down was planned. However, actually only the first two sets were of 8 reps while only 7 reps were performed in the third set. This is important information because it indicates that it is not yet time to increase the weight being used for lat-pull downs.

FIGURE 2: Example of Notebook-Type Training Log

chest press 3 x 10 @ 140, act. 3 x 10

lat pull-down 3 x 8 @ 130, act. 3 x 8, 8, 7

arm curl 2 x 8 @ 35, act. 2 x 8

triceps push-down 2 x 8 @ 45, act. 2 x 8

leg press 3 x 10 @ 200, act. 3 x 10, 10, 8

knee curl 2 x 10 @ 70, act. 2 x 10

knee extension 2 x 10 @ 80, act. 2 x 10

crunches 3 x 20 @ body weight, act. 3 x 20

Notes: time to increase weight for chest press

It is also a good idea to keep pertinent notes or comments concerning the workout in any training log. In the sample notebook log (Figure 2), it is noted that it is time to increase the weight being used for the chest press in the next workout.

How you keep a training log is not important. What is important is that you do keep a log. A training log is very important for planning future workouts and is invaluable for seeing progress and ensuring long-term success with your training program.

In this chapter we explored how to keep a log and why it is important to keep a training log. In the next chapter we will explore something that is a must for long-term weight training success and safety — proper weight training exercise technique.

Chapter *Eight*

Proper Exercise Technique

Proper exercise technique is very important for several reasons. Correct technique is needed to ensure that the muscles targeted by an exercise are indeed being trained. Incorrect technique usually results in the use of muscles to lift the weight that are not meant to be trained by an exercise. Correct technique is also needed for safe performance of the exercise. Incorrect technique many times places the lifter in an injurious situation.

There are several causes of improper exercise technique. The first one is not knowing correct technique. Obviously, if you do not know the correct technique, it is impossible to use correct technique. The second cause is improper equipment fit. This factor relates more to exercises for weight training machines than it does to free weight exercises. If you can grasp and hold a free weight, essentially the free weight bar fits you. However, on most machines such things as the seat height, seat backrest position, or position of arm or leg pads can be adjusted. If these adjustments are not made correctly, proper technique is impossible.

The last cause has to do with using too much weight for the desired number of repetitions. Often a lifter can do an exercise with correct technique until the last one or two repetitions in a set. It is important to push yourself a little when weight training, but not to the point where improper exercise technique puts you in a potentially injurious situation. For example, if you are doing back squats for a set of 8 reps, you may be able to keep your back straight and upright for the first 6 reps of the set, which is good exercise technique. During the seventh repetition you start to round your back and lean forward. Both of these are improper exercise techniques and place undue stress on your lower back, which could result in an injury. The improper technique is the result of trying to do too many repetitions with the weight being used. For long-term training success, it is better to either do fewer repetitions per set or use a lighter weight so that correct technique can be used for the entire 8 reps of the set. If you do not do one of these, there is a chance you will injure

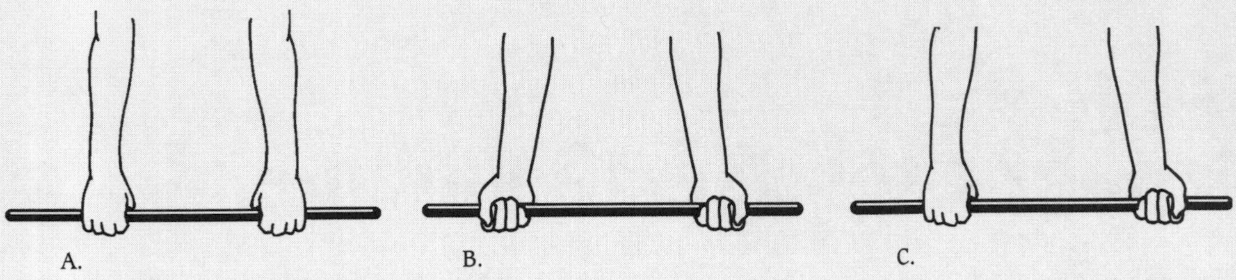

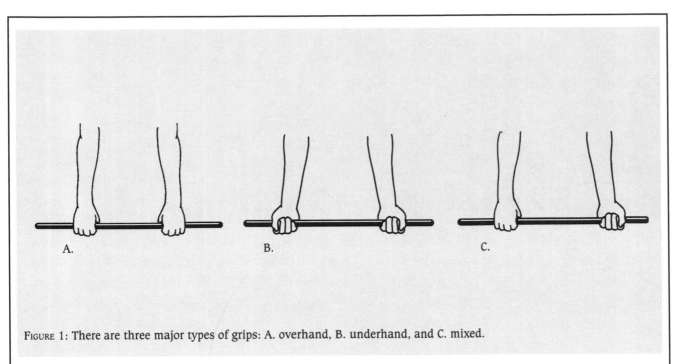

Figure 1: There are three major types of grips: A. overhand, B. underhand, and C. mixed.

yourself, which will impede the long-term success of your program.

Improper technique can also be the result of weak muscle groups. In the example of the back squat, the rounded back and leaning forward probably occur because of the abdominal and lower back muscles become fatigued as the set progresses. In this case, one way to help ensure correct technique is to do some exercises for the lower back and abdominal muscles so that they do not fatigue as quickly. In many instances of technique deterioration as a set progresses, the cause is a fatigued muscle group or groups. Strengthening the weak muscle group will do two things. First, it will allow the use of correct technique for a greater number of repetitions. Second, it will allow the use of a heavier weight for a desired number of repetitions. Therefore, if a goal of your program is to avoid injuries—and this should be a goal of all programs—or to lift more weight for a certain number of repetitions, do not use incorrect technique and do not ignore weak muscle groups in your training program.

Grips

Whether you are using free weights or weight training machines to perform many exercises, you will have to grasp a bar or handle. In most cases an overhand, or pronated, grip will be used (Figure 1). In an overhand grip, the back of the hand and knuckles are up (so that you can see them) if grasping a bar or handle that is horizontal to the floor. If grasping a handle that is vertical to the floor the back of the hand and knuckles will be facing out. The opposite of an overhand grip is an underhand, or supinated, grip. In an underhand grip the back of the hand and knuckles are down (so that you cannot see them) if grasping a bar that is horizontal to the floor. It is also possible to use a mixed, or alternate, grip. In this grip one hand uses an overhand and one an underhand grip.

Loading

Loading refers to putting weight plates or weights on a free weight bar or a machine. Loading is a very simple task but must be done correctly. In order to lift a weight plate properly from the floor or a short weight tree, lift with the legs and keep the back flat as in all lifting. This is especially true when lifting heavy weight plates. It is also important to keep a solid grip on the weight plate so that it does not slip out of your hands. So make sure to use correct technique not only during an exercise but also while loading equipment in preparation to do the exercise.

Free Weights

As discussed in Chapter 3, free weights (i.e., barbells and dumbbells) are free to move up, down, left, right, forward, and backward, making learning and performing proper exercise technique difficult. This necessitates that time be dedicated to learning proper technique before attempting to lift heavy weights for a certain number of repetitions with free weights.

It is also important to use collars when using free weights to keep the weight plates from sliding toward the end of the bar and possibly falling off of the bar. If this happens the plate may hit the lifter, a spotter, or a bystander, resulting in injury. This is especially true when performing overhead lifts. In addition, if a plate slides toward the end of a barbell or comes off completely, a twisting motion that can cause an injury may result.

The bottom line is, make sure to use collars when using free weights. This is true even for warm-up sets or sets that you consider light. It only takes one injury to prevent long-term enjoyment and success in your weight training program.

Weight Training Machines

Various aspects of weight training machines were discussed in Chapter 3. In general, because machines are free to move only in one direction, it is easier to learn correct exercise technique than when using free weights. Machines are an excellent choice when first starting to weight train because you can quickly get on with training. Later in your training program you can either decide to learn free weight exercises or continue using machines.

As mentioned before, in order to use correct exercise technique, it is necessary to adjust any machine for proper fit. Improper fit results in poor exercise technique and, potentially, an injury. All manufacturers' machines for a certain exercise, like seated knee extensions, have many things in common. For example, they must have a seat, and most are adjustable for length and backrest position, they all have a shin pad that may be adjustable for length, and they all have a resistance that can be adjusted in some way. So once you know how to adjust one manufacturer's seated knee extension machine, you pretty much know how to adjust them all. The only difference is in the location of the handles or knobs that are used to adjust each machine.

One general rule that can be applied to most single-joint weight machines is that the machine

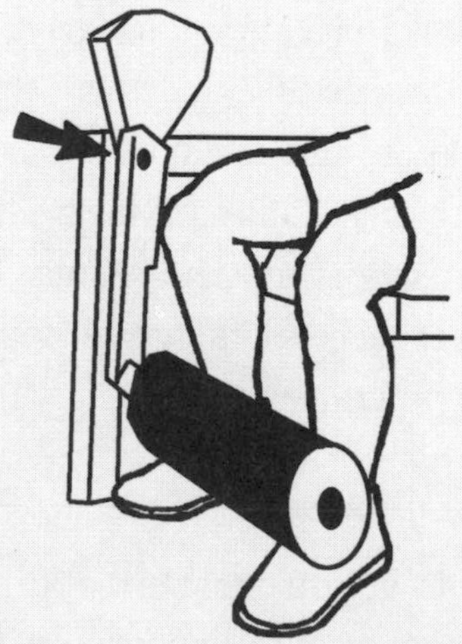

Figure 2. On most single-joint weight machines, the center of the moving joint and the center of rotation of the machine's moving part or arm must be aligned.

should be adjusted so the center of the joint that is going to move is aligned with the center of the cam, or point of rotation, of the machine. For example, let's examine the knee extension. The seat should be adjusted so that the center of rotation of the knee joint is at the center of rotation of the moving arm of the machine (Figure 2). This concept of center of a joint's rotation and center of rotation of the machine's moving part can be used to properly adjust most single-joint weight machines. In fact, some manufacturers mark with a red dot or some other marking the center of rotation of the machine's moving part in order to help you properly align yourself.

Another general rule when using any machine is that when the machine is properly adjusted, there should be no tendency for a foot, hand, arm, or other body part to lose contact with the machine. There should also be no tendency for a leg or arm to slide on a pad as the exercise is done. If there is such a tendency, it means the center of your moving joint is not aligned with the center of rotation of the machine.

Most machines are now easily adjusted. They can be adjusted to fit virtually anyone's height, leg length, and arm length. If a machine cannot be adjusted to properly fit you, do not use it. The bottom line is, know how to adjust all machines that you are going to use and take the time to adjust a machine correctly every time you use it. This will ensure good exercise technique and long-term success of your program.

Controlling the Weight

In order to get the most out of fitness weight training exercises, it is important to control the weight throughout the lifting and lowering phases of the exercise. Controlling the weight at all times ensures that the muscles are active and so will receive a training stimulus. It also helps to prevent injury. It is not necessary to count to three or four while lifting and lowering weight, but if this helps you to stay in control of the weight, then go ahead and count. The important thing to remember is to control the weight at all times.

Proper Breathing

Why it is important to breath properly and not hold your breath while weight training was discussed in detail in Chapter 4. Remember, the correct way to breathe is to inhale while lowering the weight and exhale while lifting the weight. Although holding your breath when lifting a heavy weight is natural, do not hold your breath for several continuous repetitions or continuously during one repetition.

Hand Position and Shoulder Safety

How the hands are positioned can affect how the shoulder joint is positioned. Shoulder position does affect how stable the shoulder joint is, and certain positions make the shoulder joint more prone to injury. In a normal barbell bench press, the shoulder joint is in a relatively unstable position. The instability is caused by the position of the ball on the end of the upper arm bone (humerus) in the socket of the shoulder joint. If, however, a bench press is performed with dumbbells with the palms facing each other, the shoulder position is much more stable. A general rule is that if the palms are facing each other during an exercise, the shoulder is in a more stable position than if the palms are facing forward.

This does not mean that you cannot use a palms-facing-forward position when exercising. However, if shoulder pain develops or if you have a shoulder problem, you should use a palms-facing-each-other position whenever possible. Many exercise machines have a choice of either a palms-facing-each-other or palms-facing-forward position. Use of dumbbells instead of a barbell also makes it possible to use a palms-facing-each-other instead of a palms-facing-forward position for many exercises. The choice to use a palms-facing-each-other position can help alleviate shoulder pain if it develops and should be used if you have a history of shoulder problems.

Now on to Correct Technique

There are literally hundreds of exercises and many have several variations. Thus it is impossible to include every single exercise here. Correct technique for the most common exercises used in fitness programs will be described here. General guidelines for proper exercise machine fit are also described so that you will be able to properly fit yourself to any manufacturer's piece of equipment.

Each exercise description consists of a starting position, finish position and movement, common technique errors, spotting and safety, and muscle group(s) strengthened section. Knowing common technique errors aids tremendously in avoiding them and correcting improper technique. Knowing how to spot an exercise and any other safety concern helps to ensure safety. So do not pay close attention to just the starting position, ending position, and exercise movement: know all you can about each exercise you are doing. It will help ensure long-term gains and success.

There are several exercise classification systems. A simple but useful way to classify exercises is as multi-joint and single-joint and then to further classify the exercise by muscle group trained. This type of classification makes it easy to find any exercise by knowing what muscle group it trains. Know proper exercise technique for all the exercises in your program, as exercises are the tools that make up your program.

Multi-Joint ❖ Upper Body ❖ Chest and Triceps

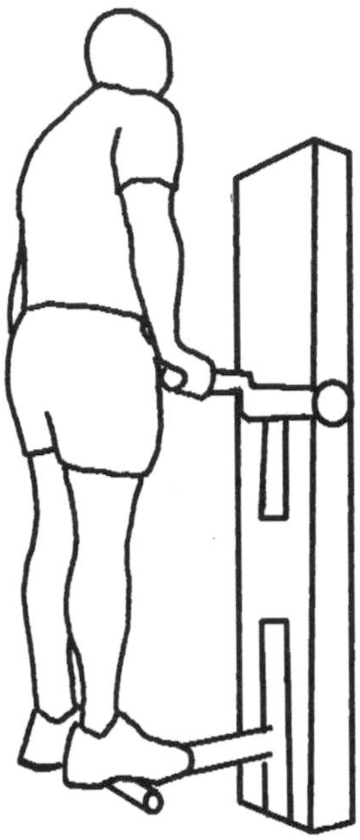

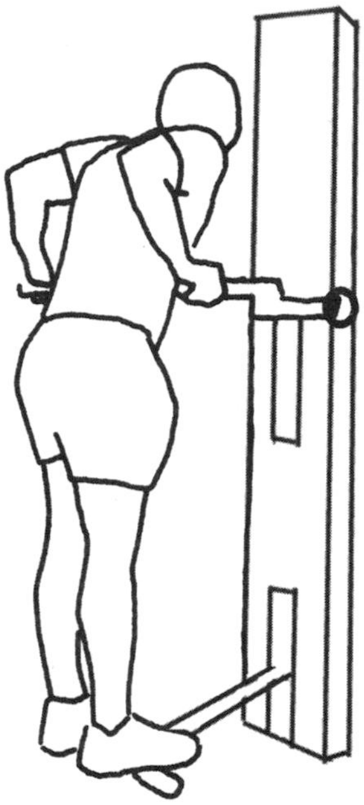

Bar Dip

Starting Position

- supporting body weight at arm's length
- torso and head upright
- hands slightly wider than shoulder width apart
- overhand grip with palms facing down and thumbs wrapped around handles
- adjust the handles to slightly wider than shoulder width apart if possible
- on some machines, it is possible to use less than body weight by standing on a movable foot plate
- on some machines, it is also possible to adjust how much assistance the foot plate gives you

Finish Position & Movement

- in a controlled manner, bend the elbows until they are at or slightly past a 90 degree angle
- then in a controlled manner, straighten the elbows and return to the starting position

Common Technique Errors

- not bending the elbows to at least a 90 degree angle

Spotting & Safety

- one spotter may assist by standing behind the lifter and placing his hands underneath the lower legs of the lifter

Muscles Strengthened

- chest area (pectoralis group), front of shoulder (anterior deltoid), back of upper arm (triceps), and upper back area (latissimus dorsi, rhomboids)

Multi-Joint ❖ Upper Body ❖ Chest and Triceps

BENCH PRESS—BARBELL

Variations

Barbell—Narrow Grip

Dumbbells

Starting Position

- lying on the back on a flat bench
- feet flat on the floor
- feet slightly wider than hip width apart
- upper back, back of head, and buttocks in contact with the bench
- barbell held at arm's length above the upper chest area
- hands wider than shoulder width apart
- overhand grip with palms facing up and forward and thumbs wrapped around the bar

Finish Position & Movement

- lower the bar in a controlled manner to mid-chest
- touch the mid-chest and then press the bar back to arm's length
- upper arms are at about a 65 degree angle to the torso during both the lowering and lifting phases
- if viewed from the side, the end of the bar will travel in a smooth arc between the arm's-length position and the chest-touch position

Multi-Joint ❖ Upper Body ❖ Chest and Triceps

Bench Press—Barbell—Narrow Grip

Starting Position

same as barbell bench press except:

- hands grasping the barbell narrower than shoulder width apart

Finish Position & Movement

same as barbell bench press except:

- upper arms are close to the torso during the entire exercise movement

Multi-Joint ❖ Upper Body ❖ Chest and Triceps

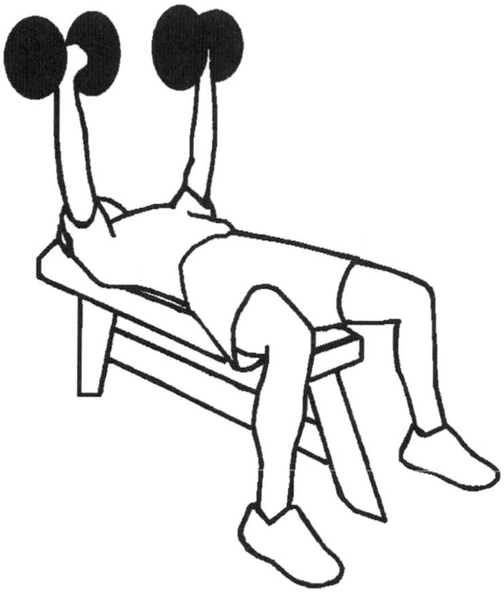

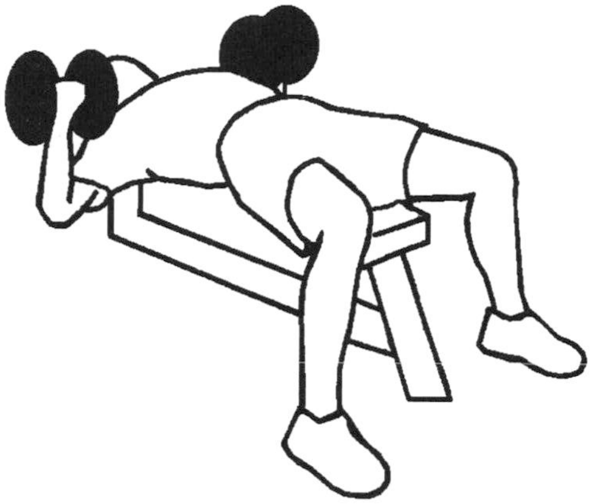

Bench Press—Dumbbells

Starting Position

the starting position is very similar to a barbell bench press except:

- dumbbells held at arm's length above the upper chest area
- dumbbells held shoulder width apart
- overhand grip with palms facing forward or each other

Finish Position & Movement

very similar to barbell bench press except:

- the dumbbells are lowered until they are at chest height then pressed back to arm's length
- if using the palms-facing-forward position, the palms can remain forward throughout the exercise or can be gradually rotated so that they are facing each other in the chest-height position and facing forward at arm's length

Common Technique Errors

Barbell and Barbell—Narrow Grip

- bouncing the barbell off of the chest, which can injure the chest area

Barbell, Barbell—Narrow Grip, and Dumbbells

- raising the hips and buttocks off of the bench (bridging) during the lifting phase, which can injure the lower back

Spotting & Safety

Barbell and Barbell—Narrow Grip

- one spotter can stand behind the head of the lifter

- if heavy weights are used, two spotters (one at each end of the barbell) should be used

Dumbbells

- two spotters (one on each side of the lifter) are recommended
- one spotter can stand behind the head of the lifter and assist by placing his or her hands underneath the lifter's elbows
- one spotter is recommended with experienced lifters only

Muscles Strengthened

Barbell, Barbell—Narrow Grip, and Dumbbells

- chest (pectoralis group), front of shoulder (anterior deltoid), and back of upper arm (triceps)

Multi-Joint ❖ Upper Body ❖ Chest and Triceps

CHEST PRESS—MACHINE

Starting Position

- seated, back flat against back of seat
- feet flat on the floor and slightly wider than hip width apart
- upper back, back of head, and buttocks in contact with the seat
- grasping the handles with an overhand grip and thumbs wrapped around handles
- adjust the seat height so that the handles are at mid-chest height when the arms are at finish position
- handles held out at arm's length
- many machines have a foot plate that can be used to assist getting the handles to arm's length

Finish Position & Movement

- in a controlled manner, let handles come back until they are even with the chest
- press the handles back to arm's length
- upper arms are at about a 65 degree angle to the torso during both the lowering and lifting phases
- keep the elbows behind the handles at all times during the exercise movement

Common Technique Errors

- raising the hips and buttocks off of the seat during the lifting phase, which can result in lower back injury

Spotting & Safety

- no spotters needed

Muscles Strengthened

- chest (pectoralis group), front of shoulder (anterior deltoid), and back of upper arm (triceps)

Multi-Joint ❖ Upper Body ❖ Chest and Triceps

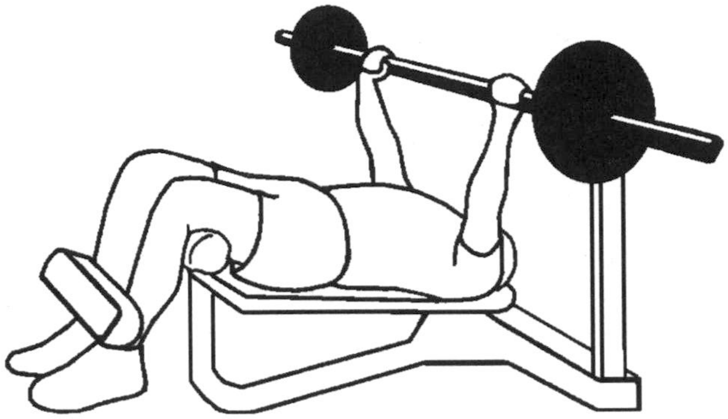

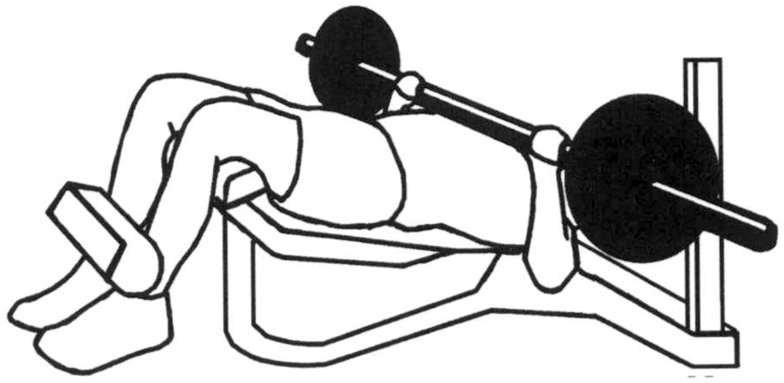

Decline Press—Barbell

Variation

Dumbbells

Starting Position

- lying on the back on a decline bench
- shins locked on the pads provided
- upper back, back of head, and buttocks in contact with the bench
- barbell held at arm's length above the lower chest area
- hands slightly wider than shoulder width apart
- overhand grip with palms facing up and forward and thumbs wrapped around the bar

Finish Position & Movement

- lower the bar in a controlled manner to the lower chest area
- touch the lower chest area and then press the barbell back to arm's length

Multi-Joint ❖ Upper Body ❖ Chest and Triceps

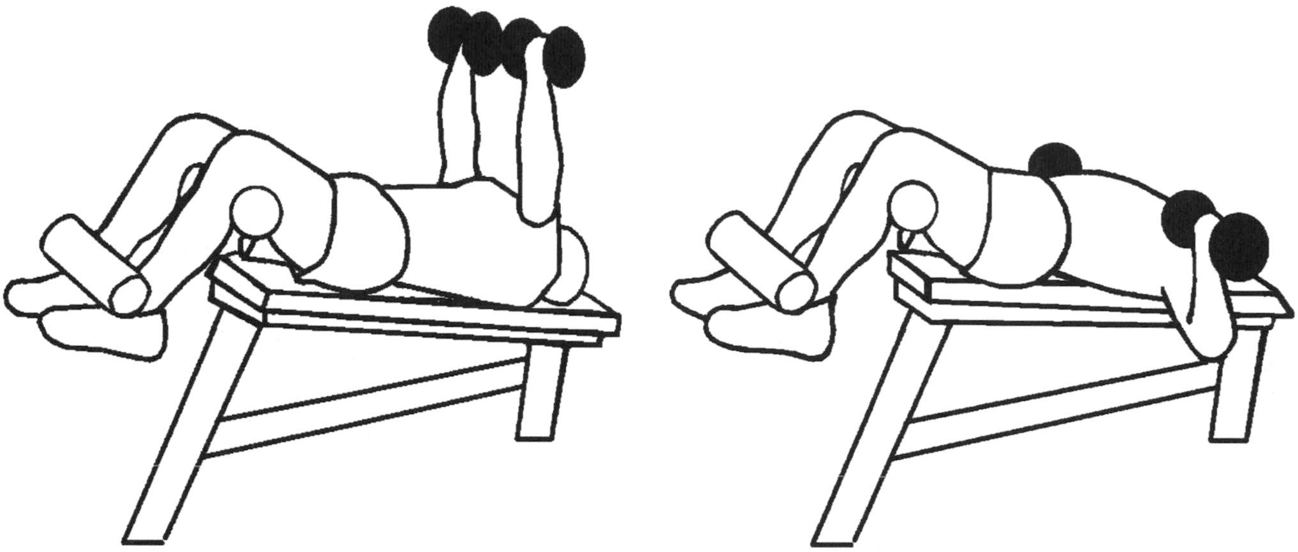

Decline Press—Dumbbells

Starting Position

same as for decline press with a barbell except:

- dumbbells held at arm's length above the lower chest area
- dumbbells held shoulder width or slightly wider than shoulder width apart
- overhand grip with palms facing up and thumbs wrapped around the dumbbell handles
- palms can be either facing each other or facing forward

Finish Position & Movement

similar to decline press with a barbell except:

- lower dumbbells until they are level with lower chest and then press dumbbells back to arm's length
- if starting with the palms facing each other, they remain so during the entire exercise movement
- if starting with the palms facing forward, they can remain forward throughout the exercise or can be gradually rotated so they are facing each other in the chest-height position and facing forward at arm's length

Common Technique Errors

Barbell and Dumbbells

- lowering the barbell or dumbbells toward the upper chest instead of the lower chest area

Dumbbells

- allowing the dumbbells to drift to the side while lowering them

Spotting & Safety

Barbell

- one spotter can stand behind the head of the lifter

Dumbbells

- one spotter can stand behind the head of the lifter and assist by placing his or her hands on the lifter's elbows
- one-spotter technique should be used with experienced lifters only
- two spotters (one on each side of the lifter) are recommended

Muscles Strengthened

Barbell and Dumbbells

- lower chest (pectoralis group), front of shoulder (anterior deltoid), and back of upper arm (triceps)

Multi-Joint ❖ Upper Body ❖ Chest and Triceps

Decline Press—Machine

Starting Position

- seated on decline press machine
- upper back, back of head, and buttocks in contact with the bench
- adjust seat height so that the handles are at lower chest level when the arms are in the finish position
- handles held at arm's length using an overhand grip
- feet flat on the floor and slightly wider than hip width apart
- some machines have handles that allow for a palms-facing-each-other and palms-facing-forward position
- many machines have a foot plate to assist in getting the handles to arm's length

Finish Position & Movement

- in a controlled manner lower the handles until they are even with the lower chest
- press handles back to arm's length
- keep the back of the head, shoulders, and buttocks in contact with the seat at all times

Common Technique Errors

- adjusting the seat height so that the handles are not at lower chest level when arms are in the finish position

Spotting & Safety

- no spotter needed

Muscles Strengthened

- lower chest (pectoralis group), front of shoulder (anterior deltoid), and back of upper arm (triceps)

Multi-Joint ❖ Upper Body ❖ Chest and Triceps

Incline Press—Barbell

Variation

Dumbbells

Starting Position

- seated on an incline bench
- back of bench is at about a 45 degree angle to the floor
- feet flat on the floor and slightly wider than hip width apart
- upper back, back of head, and buttocks in contact with the bench
- barbell held at arm's length above the upper chest and lower neck area
- hands slightly wider than shoulder width apart
- overhand grip with palms facing up and forward and thumbs wrapped around the bar

Finish Position & Movement

- lower the bar straight down in a controlled manner to the top of the breastbone (sternum)
- touch the top of the breastbone and then press the bar back to arm's length

Multi-Joint ❖ Upper Body ❖ Chest and Triceps

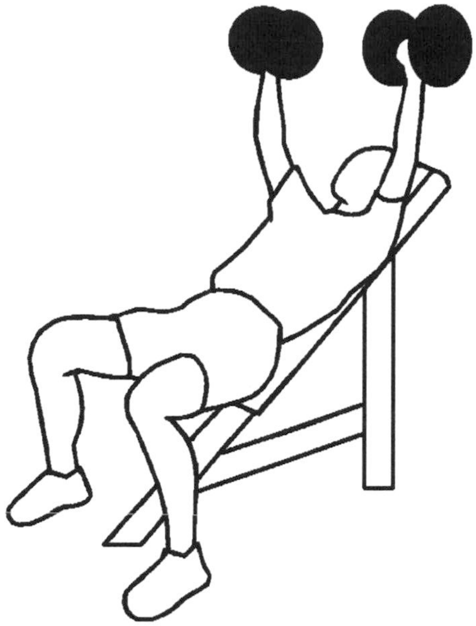

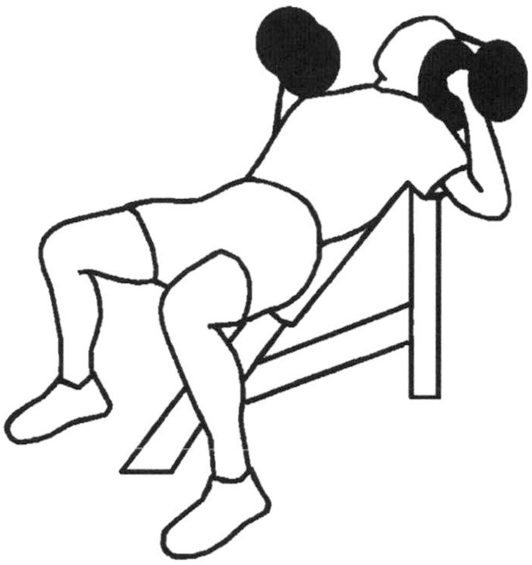

Incline Press—Dumbbells

Starting Position

same as for the incline press with a barbell except:

- dumbbells held at arm's length above the upper chest and lower neck area
- dumbbells held shoulder width or slightly wider than shoulder width apart
- overhand grip with palms facing forward or palms facing each other and thumbs wrapped around the handles of the dumbbells

Finish Position & Movement

similar to incline press with a barbell except:

- lower the dumbbells in a controlled manner until they are level with the upper chest area
- press the dumbbells back to arm's length
- if starting with the palms facing forward, they can remain facing forward throughout the exercise or they can be gradually rotated so they are facing each other in the chest-height position and facing forward at arm's length
- if starting with the palms facing each other, they remain so throughout the exercise movement

Common Technique Errors

Barbell and Dumbbells

- allowing the barbell or dumbbells to go forward during the lifting phase
- lowering the barbell or dumbbells toward mid-chest instead of the top of the breastbone (sternum)
- raising the hips and buttocks off of the bench

(bridging) during the lifting phase, which can result in lower back injury

Spotting & Safety

Barbell

- one spotter can stand behind the head of the lifter
- many incline benches have a platform on which a spotter can stand behind the head of the lifter

Dumbbells

- two spotters (one on each side of the lifter) are recommended
- with experienced lifters, one spotter can stand behind the head of the lifter and assist by placing a hand on each of the lifter's elbows

Muscles Strengthened

Barbell and Dumbbells

- chest (pectoralis group), front of shoulder (anterior deltoid), and back of upper arm (triceps)

Multi-Joint ❖ Upper Body ❖ Chest and Triceps

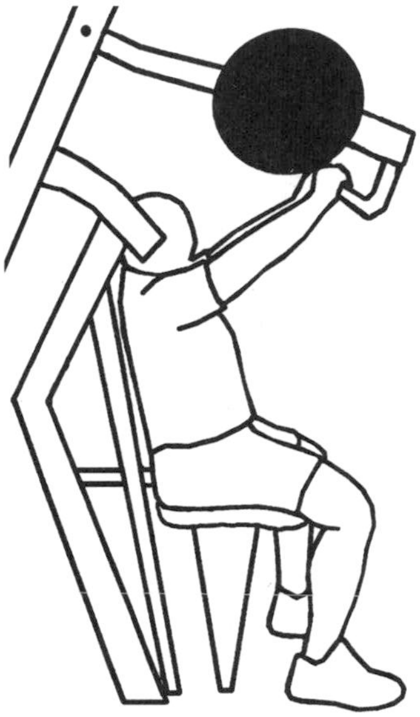

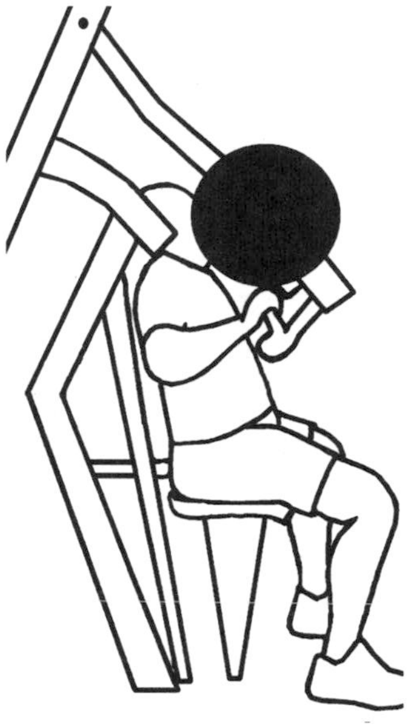

INCLINE PRESS—MACHINE

Starting Position

- seated on machine's seat
- feet flat on the floor and slightly wider than hip width apart
- upper back, back of head, and buttocks in contact with the seat
- grasping handles with an overhand grip
- some machines have handles that allow for palms-facing-each-other and palms-facing-forward positions
- handles held at arm's length
- if possible adjust the seat height so that the handles are at upper chest height when the arms are in the finish position
- many machines have a foot plate that can be pushed on to assist getting the handles into the full arm's-length position

Finish Position & Movement

- lower the handles in a controlled manner to the upper-chest position
- press handles back to arm's-length position

Common Technique Errors

- raising the hips and buttocks off of the bench (bridging) during the lifting phase, which can result in lower back injury

Spotting & Safety

- no spotter is needed

Muscles Strengthened

- chest (pectoralis group), front of shoulder (anterior deltoid), and back of upper arm (triceps)

Multi-Joint ❖ Upper Body ❖ Upper Back Musculature

Bent-Over Row—Barbell

Variation

Dumbbell

Starting Position

- standing, feet slightly wider than hip width apart and a slight bend in the knees
- bent at the waist so that the torso is almost parallel to the floor
- back is slightly arched
- neck and head in line with the rest of the back
- hands shoulder width apart
- overhand grip with palms facing the thighs and thumbs wrapped around the bar
- elbows straight and barbell held at arm's length
- shoulder blades relaxed and separated
- barbell hanging straight down from the shoulders

Finish Position & Movement

- in a controlled manner, pull the barbell upward until it touches the mid-chest area
- the pull is started by pulling the shoulder blades together and then bending at the elbows
- when the bar touches the mid-chest, the shoulder blades are still together and the elbows are higher than the back
- briefly hold the chest-touch position
- lower the barbell to the starting position by straightening the elbows and, after the elbows are straight, allowing the shoulder blades to separate
- the shoulder blades are held together during the entire pulling motion and until the end of the lowering motion
- the back should remain still throughout the entire pulling and lowering motions

Multi-Joint ❖ Upper Body ❖ Upper Back Musculature

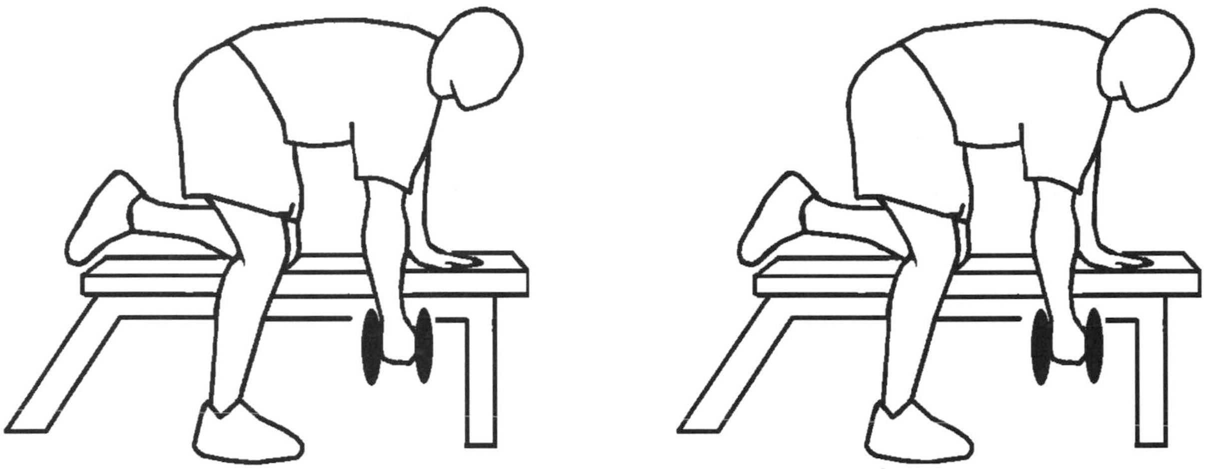

BENT-OVER ROW—DUMBBELL

Starting Position

- ♦ standing on one foot with the other leg's knee on a flat bench
- ♦ bent at the waist so that one hand is resting on the bench
- ♦ torso is about parallel to the floor
- ♦ back is slightly arched
- ♦ neck and head in line with the rest of the back
- ♦ one hand is holding a dumbbell with an overhand grip and the palm facing backward or inward
- ♦ dumbbell hanging straight down from the shoulder
- ♦ elbow straight
- ♦ dumbbell hangs down as far as possible so that the shoulder blades are separated

Finish Position & Movement

- ♦ in a controlled manner, pull the dumbbell upward until the elbow is higher than the back
- ♦ the pull is started by pulling the shoulder blades together and then bending the elbow
- ♦ the shoulder blades are held together during the entire pulling motion and until the end of the lowering motion
- ♦ briefly hold the elbow higher than the back
- ♦ lower the dumbbell to the starting position by straightening the elbow and, after the elbow is straight, allowing the shoulder blades to separate
- ♦ the back should remain still throughout the entire pulling and lowering motions
- ♦ if starting with the palm facing backward, it

can remain facing backward throughout the motion or the palm can gradually rotate so that it faces inward at the top of the pull and then again faces backward at the end of the lowering phase

- if starting with the palm facing inward, it can remain so throughout the entire exercise movement

Common Technique Errors

Barbell

- using the back and legs to start the lifting movement, which can result in lower back injury
- raising the torso so that it is not parallel to floor
- not pulling the shoulder blades together

Dumbbells

- rotating back to start the lifting movement, which can result in lower back injury
- not pulling the shoulder blades together

Spotting & Safety

Barbell and Dumbbells

- no spotter is needed

Muscles Strengthened

Barbell and Dumbbells

- upper back (trapezius, rhomboids), lats (latissimus dorsi), back of shoulder (posterior deltoid), and elbow flexors (front of upper arm, biceps, brachialis)

Multi-Joint ❖ Upper Body ❖ Upper Back Musculature

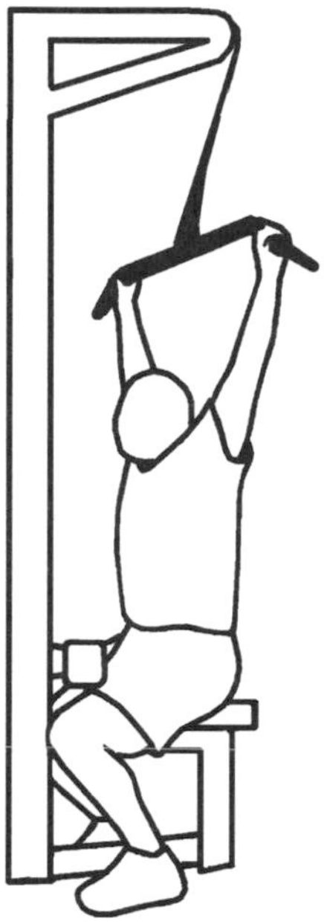

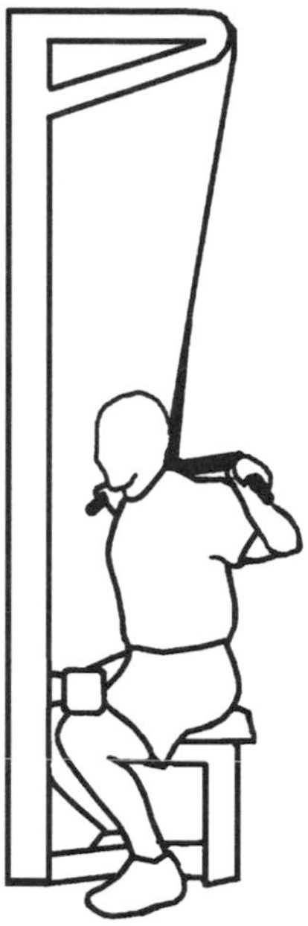

Lat Pull-Down

Starting Position

- seated, with thighs under the thigh pads
- if possible adjust the height of the thigh pads so that they hold you down when seated
- feet flat on the floor
- overhand grip with the hands at least shoulder width apart
- palms facing forward
- elbows straight
- neck and head in line with the rest of the back
- back straight
- move forward or back so that the handle can be pulled straight down to the front of the shoulders
- several different types of handles can be used

Finish Position & Movement

- in a controlled manner, pull the handle and touch the front of the shoulders
- the pull is started by pulling the shoulder blades down, followed by pulling with the arms
- briefly hold the handle in the lowest position
- in a controlled fashion, return the handle to the starting position
- the return motion is started by straightening the elbows followed by allowing the shoulders to elevate
- the back and legs stay still during the entire motion

Common Technique Errors

- leaning back to start the lifting movement
- not pulling with the shoulder blades
- pulling the bar to the back of the shoulders places shoulders in an injurious position

Spotting & Safety

- no spotter is needed

Muscles Strengthened

- lats (latissimus dorsi), upper back (trapezius, rhomboids), and elbow flexors (biceps, brachialis)

Multi-Joint ❖ Upper Body ❖ Upper Back Musculature

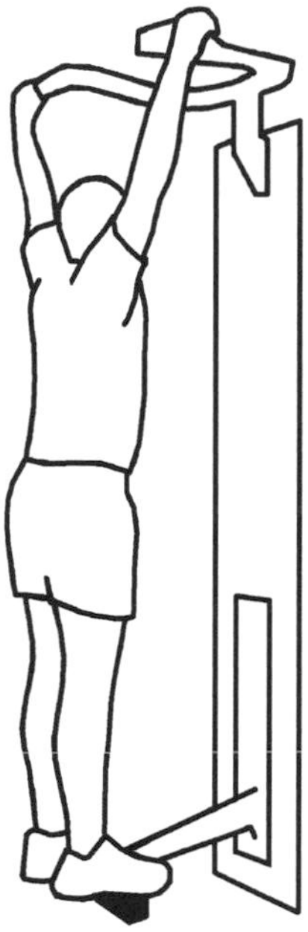

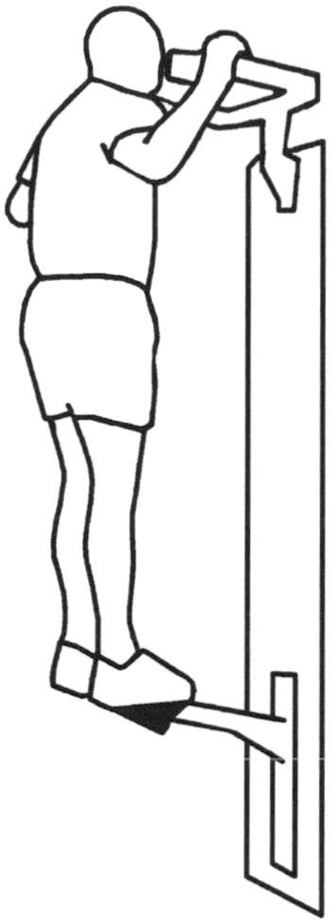

Pull-Up

Starting Position

- overhand grip with the palms facing forward
- hands at least shoulder width apart
- entire body hanging straight down
- some pull-up machines have a foot plate that can be stood on while doing the exercise
- on some machines the force of the foot plate makes it possible to do the exercise with less than body weight as resistance

Finish Position & Movement

- in a controlled manner, pull the body up until the chin is above the bar
- hold the chin above the bar briefly, and then in a controlled manner, return to the starting position
- the back and legs stay still during the entire motion

Common Technique Errors

- raising the legs to help the start of the pulling motion
- not getting the chin above the bar

Spotting & Safety

- a spotter can assist from behind by grasping the lifter at the waist

Muscles Strengthened

- lats (latissimus dorsi), upper back (trapezius, rhomboids), back of shoulder (posterior deltoid), and elbow flexors (biceps, brachialis)

Multi-Joint ❖ Upper Body ❖ Upper Back Musculature

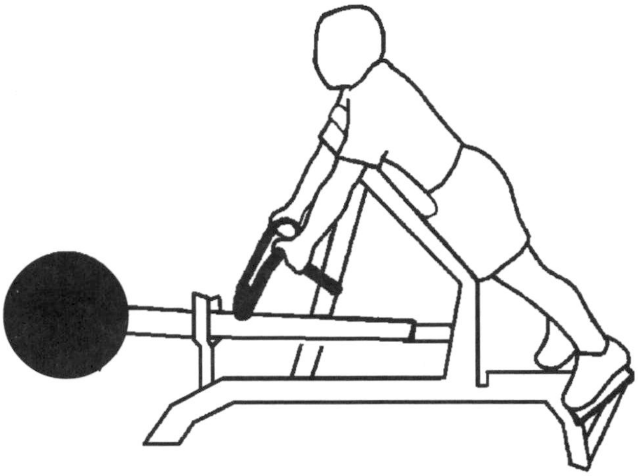

T-Bar Row

Starting Position

- leaning forward so that the chest is resting on the chest pad of the T-bar row machine
- feet flat on the foot plates and hip width apart
- knees slightly bent
- lower and upper back straight and slightly arched
- neck and head in line with the rest of the back
- overhand grip on the handles
- some machines allow for either a palms-facing-each-other or a palms-facing-backward grip
- elbows straight and handles held at arm's length
- shoulder blades relaxed and separated
- handles hanging down from the shoulder
- if possible, adjust foot plates so that chest plate is in contact with entire breastbone (sternum)

Finish Position & Movement

- in a controlled manner, pull the handles upward as far as possible
- the pull is started by pulling the shoulder blades together and then bending at the elbows
- when the handles are as high as possible, the shoulder blades are still together and the elbows are slightly higher than the back
- briefly hold the handles in their highest position
- in a controlled manner, lower the handles to the starting position by straightening the elbows and, after the elbows are straight, allowing the shoulder blades to separate
- after the shoulder blades are pulled together, they remain that way for the entire pulling

phase, until the end of the lowering motion

- the back should remain still throughout the entire pulling and lowering motions

Common Technique Errors

- using the back to start the lifting movement, which can result in lower back injury
- not pulling the shoulder blades together

Spotting & Safety

- no spotter is needed

Muscles Strengthened

- upper back (trapezius, rhomboids), lats (latissimus dorsi), back of shoulder (posterior deltoid), and elbow flexors (front of upper arm, biceps, brachialis)

Multi-Joint ❖ Upper Body ❖ Upper Back Musculature

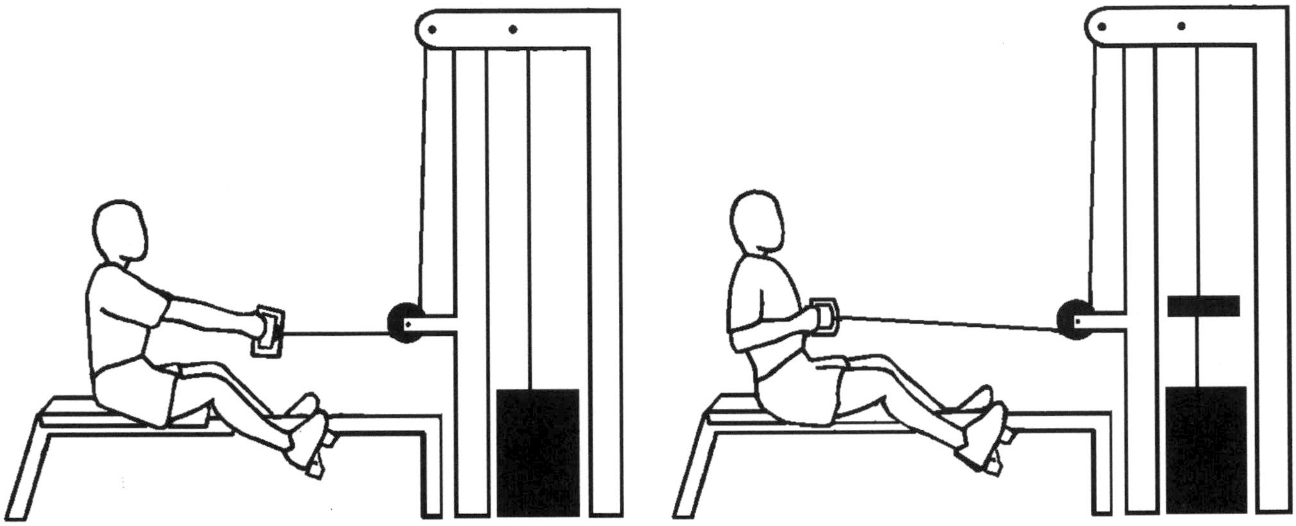

Seated Row—Cable

Starting Position

- seated, with the torso forming a 90 degree angle with the legs
- feet flat on the foot plates and hip width apart
- knees slightly bent
- lower and upper back straight and slightly arched
- neck and head in line with the rest of the back
- overhand grip
- there are many types of handles that can be used for this exercise
- elbows straight and handles held at arm's length
- shoulder blades relaxed and separated
- if possible, adjust the length of cable so that resistance is felt in the starting position

Finish Position & Movement

- in a controlled manner, pull the handles backward until touching the chest
- the pull is started by pulling the shoulder blades together and then bending at the elbows
- when the handles touch the chest, the shoulder blades are still together and the elbows are slightly behind the back
- briefly hold the handles to the chest
- in a controlled manner, return the handles to the starting position by straightening the elbows and, after the elbows are straight, allowing the shoulder blades to separate
- once the shoulder blades are together, they remain so during the entire pulling and arm straightening motions

- the back should remain still throughout the entire pulling and arm straightening motions

Common Technique Errors

- using the back to start the lifting movement, which can result in lower back injury
- not pulling the shoulder blades together

Spotting & Safety

- no spotter is needed

Muscles Strengthened

- upper back (trapezius, rhomboids), lats (latissimus dorsi), back of shoulder (posterior deltoid), and elbow flexors (front of upper arm, biceps, brachialis)

Multi-Joint ❖ Upper Body ❖ Upper Back Musculature

Seated Row—Machine

Starting Position

- seated, with the chest in contact with the chest plate
- feet flat on the floor and slightly wider than hip width apart
- lower and upper back straight and slightly arched
- neck and head in line with the rest of the back
- overhand grip
- some machines have handles that allow palms-facing-each-other and palms-facing-downward positions
- elbows straight and handles held at arm's length
- shoulder blades relaxed and separated
- if possible, adjust the seat height so that the chest plate is in contact with the entire breastbone (sternum)

Finish Position & Movement

- in a controlled manner, pull the handles backward as far as possible
- the pull is started by pulling the shoulder blades together and then bending at the elbows
- when the handles are as far back as possible, the shoulder blades are still together and the elbows are slightly behind the back
- briefly hold the handles in the farthest-back position
- in a controlled manner, return the handles to the starting position by straightening the

elbows and, after the elbows are straight, allowing the shoulder blades to separate

- once the shoulder blades are together, they remain so during the entire pulling and arm straightening motions
- the back should remain still throughout the entire arm pulling and straightening motions

Common Technique Errors

- using the back to start the lifting movement, which can result in lower back injury
- not pulling the shoulder blades together

Spotting & Safety

- no spotter is needed

Muscles Strengthened

- upper back (trapezius, rhomboids), lats (latissimus dorsi), back of shoulder (posterior deltoid), and elbow flexors (front of upper arm, biceps, brachialis)

Multi-Joint ❖ Upper Body ❖ Shoulders and Triceps

Overhead Press—Barbells

Variation

Dumbbells

Starting Position

- standing, with feet slightly wider than hip width apart and feet slightly staggered front to back for balance
- torso upright, head upright, and a slight bend in the knees
- barbell held touching the upper breastbone (sternum)
- hands slightly wider than shoulder width apart
- overhand grip with palms facing upward
- elbows directly below the bar
- the barbell can be taken from a power rack to get into the starting position

Finish Position & Movement

- in a controlled manner, press the bar straight up until it is at arm's length
- briefly hold the bar at arm's length and, in a controlled manner, return to the starting position
- elbows remain directly below the bar throughout the movement
- a slight bend of the knees can be used to cushion the stopping of the bar at the top of the breastbone at the end of the lowering phase

Multi-Joint ❖ Upper Body ❖ Shoulders and Triceps

Overhead Press—Dumbbell

Starting Position

same as for the overhead press with a barbell except:

- dumbbells held at shoulder height
- hands shoulder width apart
- overhand grip with palms facing upward and forward or upward and toward each other

Finish Position & Movement

similar to the overhead press with a barbell except:

- press the dumbbells straight up until they are at arm's length
- briefly hold dumbbells at arm's length and, in a controlled manner, return to starting position
- the dumbbells can be lifted both at once or in an alternating arm fashion
- if starting with the palms facing forward, they can remain so throughout the exercise movement or they can be gradually rotated so that they face each other when the arms are straight and face forward when at shoulder height

Common Technique Errors

Barbell and Dumbbells

- using the legs to start the lifting motion
- not keeping the elbows below the barbell or dumbbells at the start of the lifting motion
- allowing the barbell or dumbbells to go forward and not straight up during the lifting motion

Spotting & Safety

Barbell and Dumbbells

- two spotters (one on each side of the lifter) are recommended

Muscles Strengthened

Barbell and Low Pulley

- front of shoulder (anterior deltoid) and back of upper arm (triceps)

Multi-Joint ❖ Upper Body ❖ Shoulders and Triceps

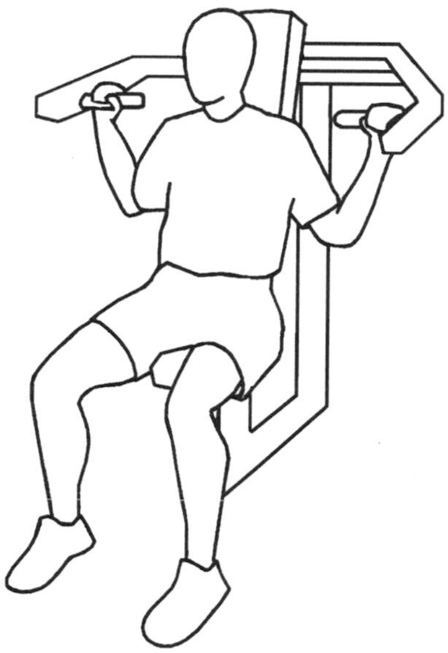

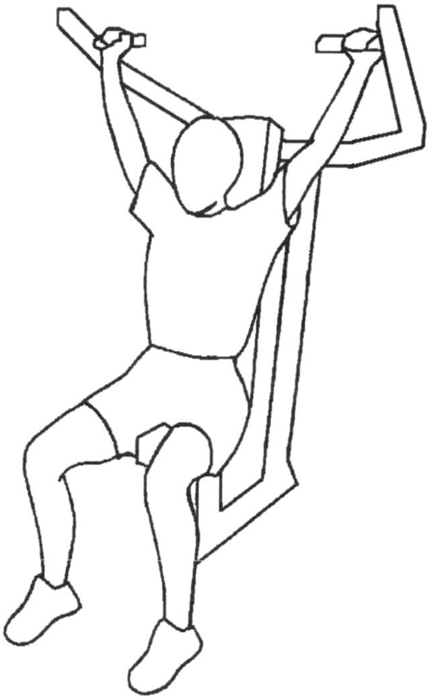

Overhead Press—Machine

Starting Position

- seated, with back and head against the seat back
- feet are either flat on the floor and slightly wider than hip width apart or hanging from the seat
- adjust the seat height so that the handles are level with the upper shoulder
- tighten the seat belt if provided
- overhand grip with thumbs wrapped around the handle
- elbows directly below the handles
- some machines allow for palms-facing-forward and palms-facing-each-other positions

Finish Position & Movement

- in a controlled manner, press the handles to arm's length
- briefly hold the handles at arm's length and then return to the starting position
- elbows remain directly below handles at all times
- keep back and back of head in contact with seat back at all times

Common Technique Errors

- not keeping the elbows below the handles at the start of the lifting motion
- bouncing weights out of lowest position after completion of a repetition to start the next repetition

Spotting & Safety

- no spotters are needed

Muscles Strengthened

- front of shoulder (anterior deltoid) and back of upper arm (triceps)

Multi-Joint ❖ Upper Body ❖ Shoulders

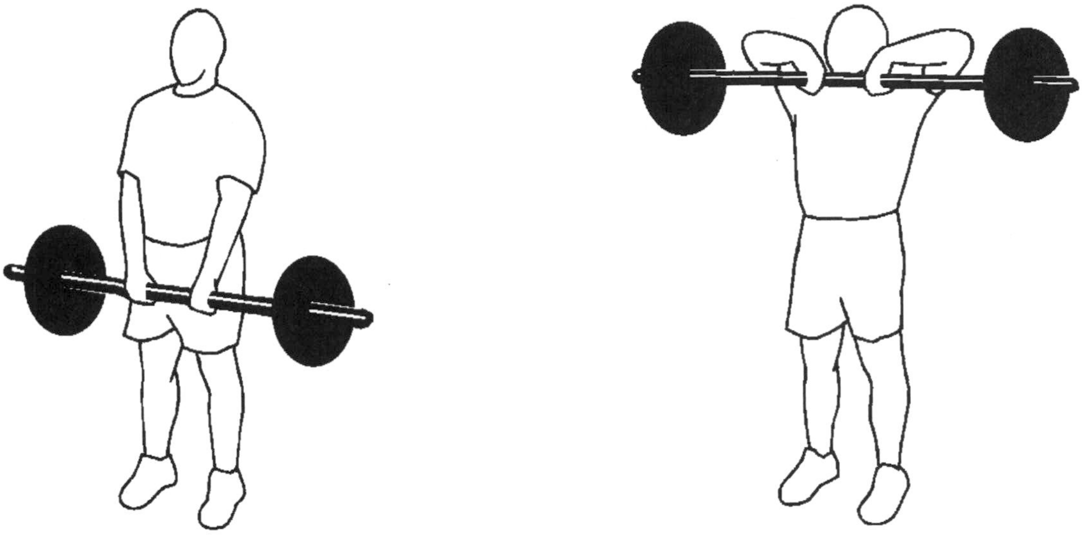

Upright Row—Barbell

Variation

Low Pulley

Starting Position

- standing, with feet slightly wider than hip width apart and knees slightly bent
- overhand grip on barbell
- hands six inches or wider apart and palms facing the thighs
- elbows straight and barbell touching the thighs
- back straight and shoulders back
- neck and head in line with the rest of the back

Finish Position & Movement

- in a controlled manner, pull the barbell up to shoulder height
- the elbows stay above the bar at all times during the exercise
- the bar is pulled straight up along the body
- briefly hold the barbell at shoulder height
- in a controlled fashion, return barbell to starting position
- the back and legs stay still during the entire motion

Multi-Joint ❖ Upper Body ❖ Shoulders

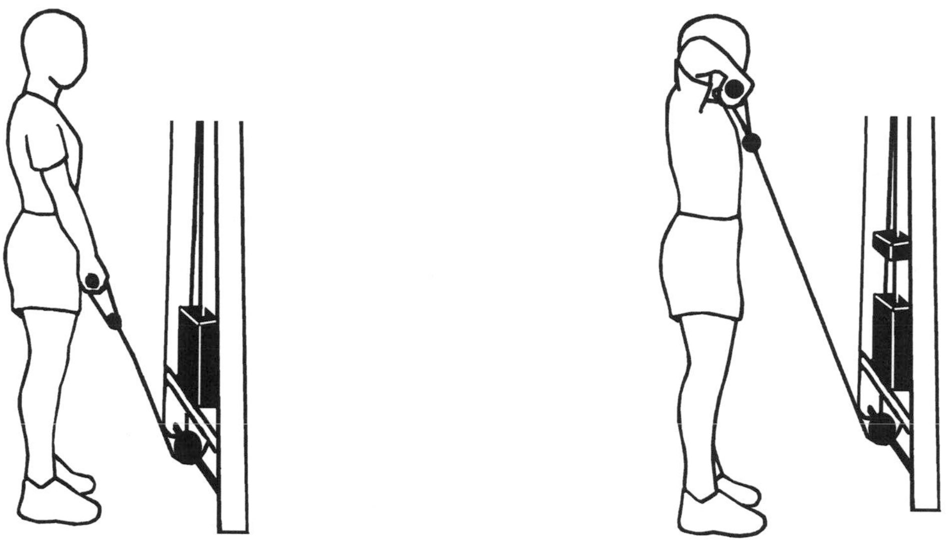

Upright Row—Low Pulley

Starting Position

similar to the upright row with a barbell except:

- standing close to the low pulley so that the handle can be pulled nearly straight up

Finish Position & Movement

similar to the upright row with a barbell except:

- pull the handle attached to the low pulley up to shoulder height
- return the handle to the starting position

Common Technique Errors

Barbell and Low Pulley

- using the back to start the lifting movement, which can result in lower back injury

Spotting & Safety

Barbell and Low Pulley

- no spotter is needed

Muscles Strengthened

Barbell and Low Pulley

- entire shoulder area (deltoid), upper back (trapezius, rhomboids), and elbow flexors (front of upper arm, biceps, brachialis)

Single-Joint ❖ Chest

Dumbbell Fly—Flat Bench

Variations

Decline Bench

Incline Bench

Starting Position

- lying on the back on a flat bench with feet flat on the floor
- back of the head lying on the bench
- using an overhand grip, hold dumbbells in each hand directly above the chest
- palms facing each other
- elbows slightly bent

Finish Position & Movement

- moving at the shoulder in a controlled manner, lower both dumbbells to the side
- lower the dumbbells until upper arm is parallel to the floor
- in a controlled manner, return to the starting position
- when arms are parallel to the floor the palms face upward
- do not rotate forearms or shoulders during the motion
- the slight bend in the elbows should be maintained throughout the exercise motion
- the back and head should maintain contact with the bench at all times
- the feet should remain flat on the floor at all times

Single-Joint ❖ Chest

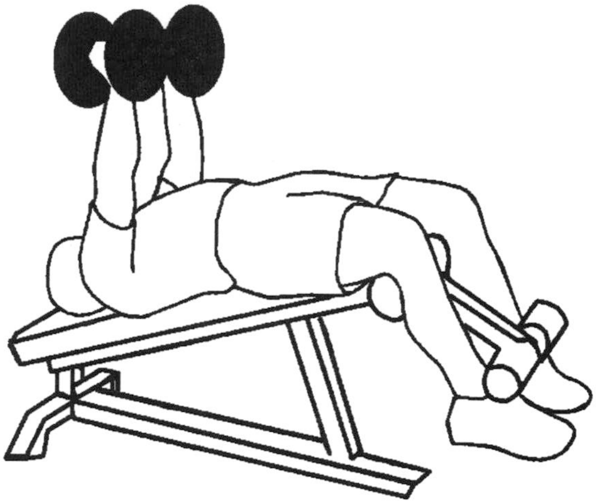

Dumbbell Fly—Decline Bench

Starting Position

same as dumbbell fly with a flat bench except:

- lying on the back on a decline bench with the shins hooked over the pads provided

Finish Position & Movement

same as dumbbell fly with a flat bench

Single-Joint ❖ Chest

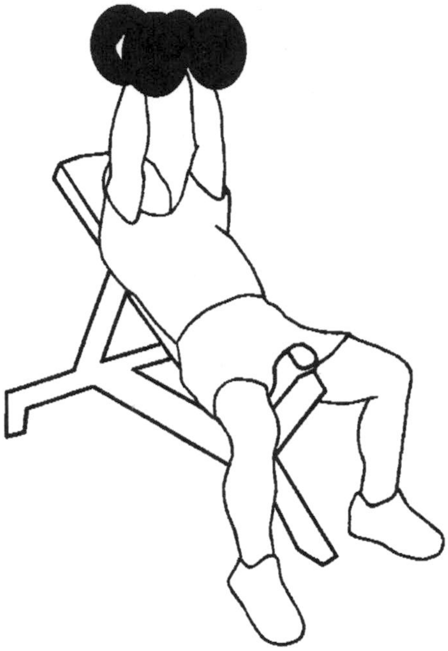

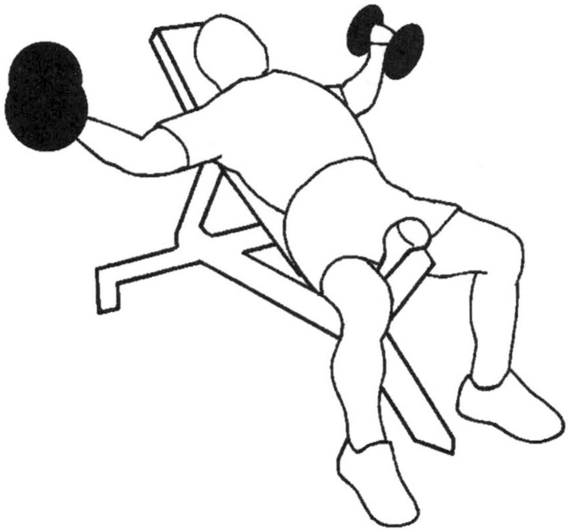

Dumbbell Fly—Incline Bench

Starting Position

same as dumbbell fly with a flat bench except:

- lying on the back on an incline bench with feet flat on the floor

Finish Position & Movement

same as dumbbell fly with a flat bench

Common Technique Errors

Flat Bench, Decline Bench, and Incline Bench

- raising the head or back off the bench

Spotting & Safety

Flat Bench, Decline Bench, and Incline Bench

- a spotter can hand the dumbbells to the lifter once the lifter is in the starting position
- a spotter can take the dumbbells from the lifter after the completion of a set
- a spotter can kneel at the head of the lifter and assist by placing his or her hands underneath the elbows of the lifter (this is recommended with experienced lifters only)
- two spotters are recommended (one spotting each arm) for inexperienced lifters

Muscles Strengthened

Flat Bench, Decline Bench, and Incline Bench

- entire chest area (pectoralis group)

Decline Bench

- emphasizes lower chest area

Incline Bench

- emphasizes upper chest area

Single-Joint ❖ Chest

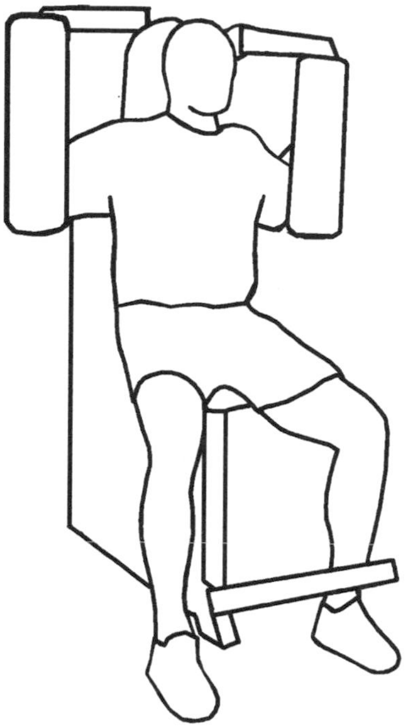

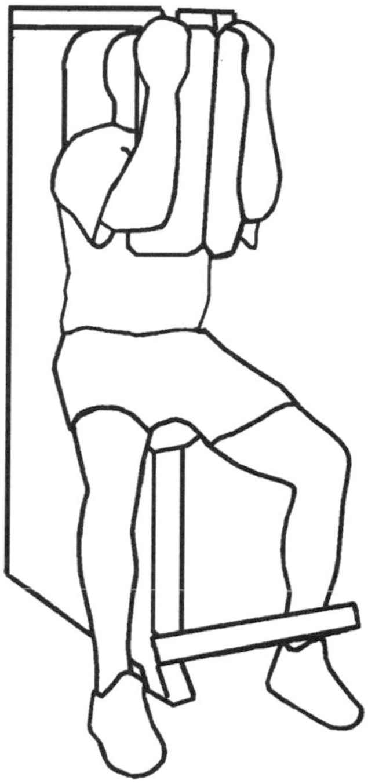

Pec Deck

Starting Position

- seated with the back and head in contact with the back of the seat
- adjust seat so that the middle of the shoulders, as viewed from the top, are in line with the center of rotation of the machine's cams
- correct seat height places the upper arm in a position that is parallel to the floor
- place elbows on the pads provided and loosely grip the handles (if provided)
- the elbows form about a 90 degree angle
- with most machines, the feet are flat on the floor

Finish Position & Movement

- push the elbow pads forward until they meet in front of the middle of the chest
- in a controlled manner, return to the starting position
- force during the movement should be applied with the elbows and not the hands
- the back and head should maintain contact with the bench at all times
- the feet should remain flat on the floor at all times

Common Technique Errors

- applying most of the force with the hands and not the elbows, which allows use of the anterior deltoid, located on the front of the shoulder
- moving the head or back off of the bench

Spotting & Safety

- no spotting is needed

Muscles Strengthened

- entire chest area (pectoralis group)

Single-Joint ❖ Shoulder

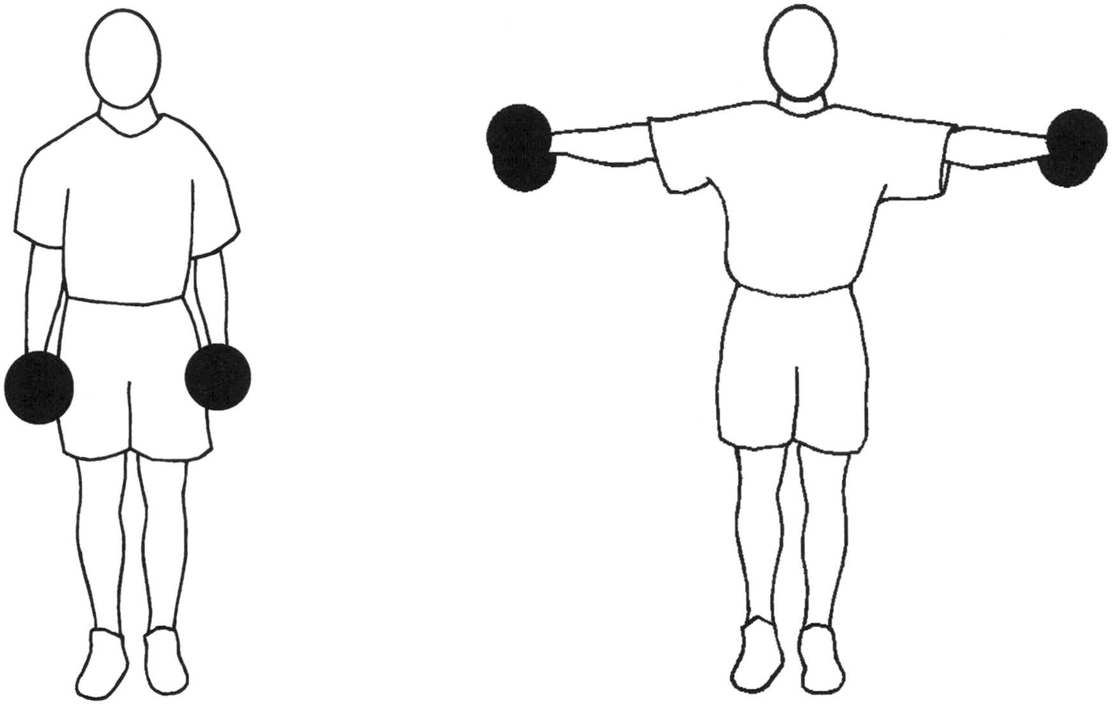

Lateral Shoulder Raise—Dumbbells

Variation

Front Shoulder Raise

Starting Position

- standing
- holding a dumbbell in each hand with an overhand grip
- palms facing the thighs
- arms hanging at the sides
- elbows slightly bent
- feet hip width apart
- slight bend in the knees
- head upright

Finish Position & Movement

- in a controlled manner, raise both dumbbells out to the side
- raise dumbbells until arms are parallel to the floor
- briefly hold dumbbells parallel to floor
- in a controlled manner, return to starting position
- keep palms facing the thighs at all times
- palms face the floor when arms are parallel to the floor
- elbows remain slightly bent throughout entire movement

Single-Joint ❖ Shoulder

FRONT SHOULDER RAISE—DUMBBELLS

Starting Position

same as for lateral shoulder raise with a dumbbell

Finish Position & Movement

same as for lateral shoulder raise with dumbbells except:

- can be performed using both arms at once or in an alternate arm fashion
- in a controlled manner, raise the dumbbell(s) to the front
- raise the dumbbell(s) until the arm(s) are parallel to the floor
- briefly hold the dumbbell(s) parallel to floor
- in a controlled manner, return to starting position
- elbows remain slightly bent throughout the entire movement

Common Technique Errors

Lateral and Front Shoulder Raise

- using the legs, back, or other muscles to start the lifting of the dumbbell(s)
- rolling shoulders so that palms do not face the thighs but toward the front; this places more training stress on the front of the shoulder and less on the middle of the shoulder

Spotting & Safety

Lateral and Front Shoulder Raise

- no spotting needed

Muscles Strengthened

Lateral Shoulder Raise

- entire deltoid

Front Shoulder Raise

- emphasizes front part of shoulder (anterior deltoid)

Single-Joint ❖ Shoulder

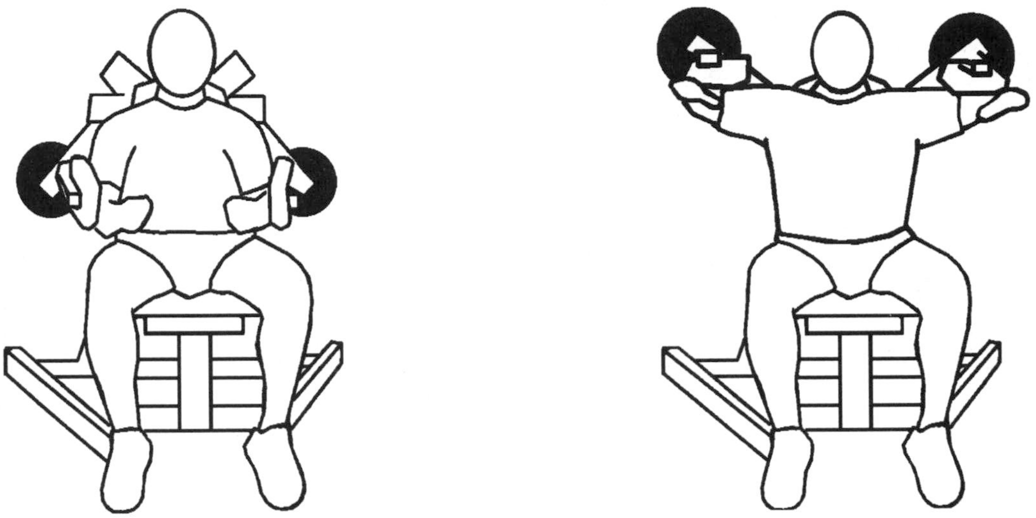

Lateral Shoulder Raise—Machine

Starting Position

- adjust the seat height so that the shoulders are centered on the middle of the cam or pulley
- place the upper arm and/or elbow on pads
- palms facing the torso
- elbows bent at a 90 degree angle
- feet flat on the floor or hanging down on some machines
- torso upright and chest out
- head upright

Finish Position & Movement

- in a controlled manner, raise upper arms to the sides
- push on the pads with upper arm or elbow area
- raise upper arms until parallel to the floor
- hold upper arms parallel to floor for 1 to 2 seconds
- in a controlled manner, return to starting position
- keep palms facing the torso at all times
- elbows remain at 90 degree angle throughout the entire movement

Common Technique Errors

- using the legs, back, or other muscles to start the lifting motion
- rolling shoulders backward so that palms do not face the torso but toward the front with fingers pointing toward the ceiling; this places more training stress on the front of the shoulder and less on the middle of the shoulder

Spotting & Safety

- no spotting needed

Muscles Strengthened

- entire deltoid

Single-Joint ❖ Trapezius

Shoulder Shrug—Barbell

Variation

Dumbbells

Machine

Starting Position

- standing
- holding a barbell with hands shoulder width apart
- use an overhand grip with palms facing the thighs
- shoulders hanging as low as possible
- elbows straight
- feet hip width apart
- slight bend in the knees
- head upright and looking forward

Finish Position & Movement

- in a controlled manner, raise the shoulders as high as possible and try and touch the ears with both shoulders
- briefly hold the highest shoulder position
- return to the starting position in a controlled manner
- keep the elbows straight throughout the movement
- keep head upright and looking forward at all times

Common Technique Errors

- using the legs, back, or other muscles to start the lifting motion
- tilting the head back and looking at the ceiling, which limits the range of motion

Spotting & Safety

- no spotting needed

Muscles Strengthened

- upper back and back of neck
- predominantly the trapezius

Single-Joint ❖ Trapezius

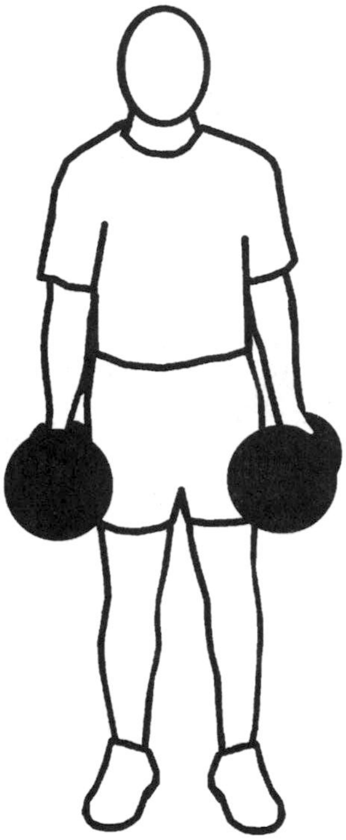

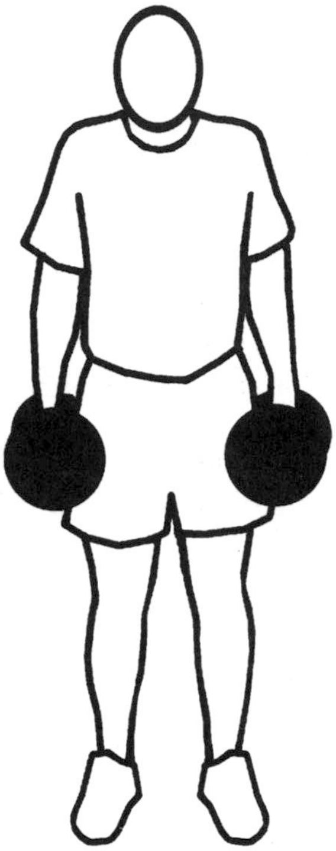

Shoulder Shrug—Dumbbells

Starting Position

same as for shoulder shrug with a barbell except:

- using an overhand grip, hold a dumbbell in each hand
- palms face the thighs

Finish Position & Movement

same as for shoulder shrug with a barbell except:

- the palms face the sides at all times throughout the exercise movement

Common Technique Errors

- using the legs, back, or other muscles to start the lifting motion
- tilting the head back and looking at the ceiling, which limits the range of motion

Spotting & Safety

- no spotting needed

Muscles Strengthened

- upper back and back of neck
- predominantly the trapezius

Single-Joint ❖ Trapezius

Shoulder Shrug—Machine

Starting Position

- adjust seat height so that the shoulders can hang down as far as possible
- grasping the handles with an overhand grip
- arms straight
- feet flat on the floor
- head upright and looking forward

Finish Position & Movement

- in a controlled manner, raise the shoulders as high as possible and try and touch the ears with both shoulders
- briefly hold the highest shoulder position
- return to the starting position in a controlled manner
- keep head upright and looking forward at all times

Common Technique Errors

- using the legs, back, or other muscles to start the lifting motion
- tilting the head back and looking at the ceiling, which limits the range of motion

Spotting & Safety

- no spotting needed

Muscles Strengthened

- upper back and back of neck
- predominantly the trapezius

Single-Joint ❖ Triceps (Back of Upper Arm)

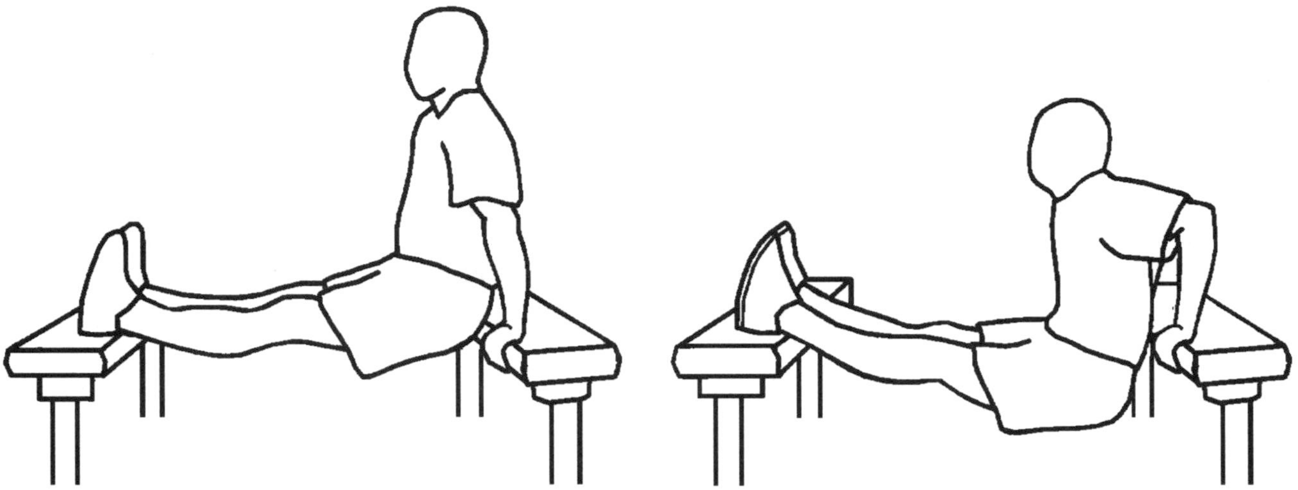

Bench Dip

Starting Position

- adjust the distance between two flat benches so that the heels are on one bench and the palms of the hands on the other
- the elbows are straight
- palms are flat on one bench with the fingers pointing forward
- hands are slightly wider than shoulder width apart
- torso is upright and forms a 90 degree angle with the legs
- head is upright and looking forward

Finish Position & Movement

- bend at the elbows until the buttocks touch or almost touch the floor
- return to the starting position in a controlled manner by straightening the elbows
- lower arms should remain perpendicular to the floor throughout the entire movement

Common Technique Errors

- pushing with the legs to return to the starting position

Spotting & Safety

- no spotter is normally needed
- one spotter can stand behind the lifter and assist by placing his or her hands in the lifter's armpits
- be sure benches are sturdy and will not slide

Muscles Strengthened

- back of upper arm (triceps), front of shoulder (anterior deltoid), chest (pectoralis group), and upper back (latissimus dorsi, rhomboids)

Single-Joint ❖ Triceps (Back of Upper Arm)

Triceps Kickback—Dumbbell

Starting Position

- using an overhand grip, grasp a dumbbell in one hand with the palm facing the thigh
- upper arm is parallel to the floor
- elbow is at 90 degrees
- place the opposite hand and knee on a bench, which should place the back in a position that is about parallel to the floor
- head is upright and looking slightly forward

Finish Position & Movement

- moving only at the elbow in a controlled manner, straighten the elbow until it is completely straight
- hold the straightened-elbow position briefly and, in a controlled manner, return to the starting position
- the elbow, shoulder, and upper arm should remain stationary throughout the exercise movement

Common Technique Errors

- moving the shoulder, upper arm, or elbow to start lifting the dumbbell

Spotting & Safety

- no spotting needed

Muscles Strengthened

- back of upper arm (triceps)
- especially lateral and medial head of triceps

Single-Joint ❖ Triceps (Back of Upper Arm)

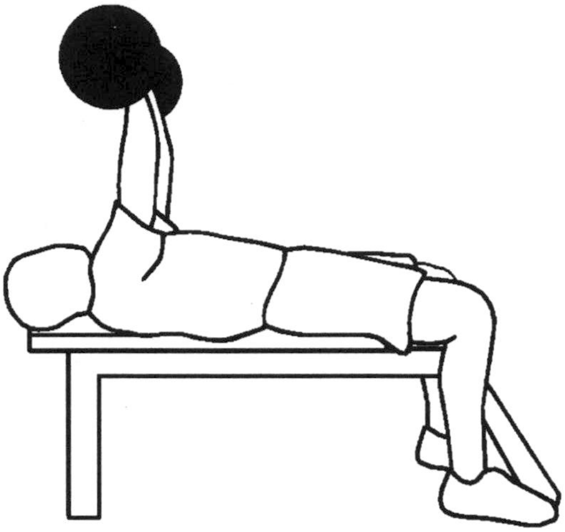

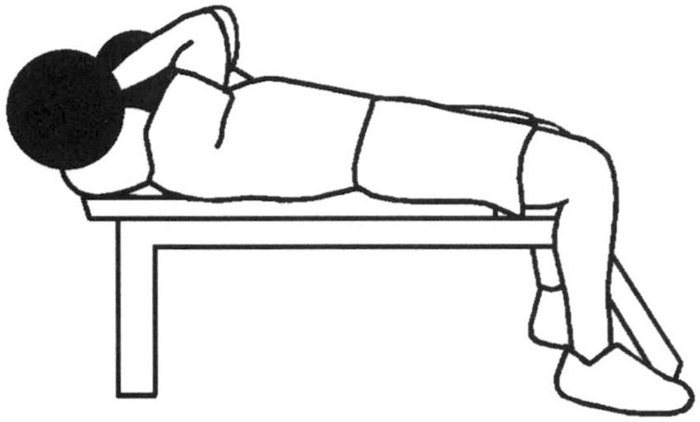

Triceps Extension—Lying EZ Curl Bar

Variation

Lying Dumbbell

Starting Position

- lying on the back on a flat bench
- use an overhand grip to grasp an EZ curl bar barbell so that the little fingers are higher than the thumbs
- palms facing upward
- hands slightly narrower than shoulder width apart
- holding the EZ curl bar above the chest with arms fully extended
- feet flat on the floor

Finish Position & Movement

- bending only at the elbows and in a controlled manner, lower barbell toward the forehead
- lower the EZ curl bar until it almost touches the forehead
- stop briefly at the lowest position
- in a controlled manner, return to the starting position by straightening the elbows
- elbows, shoulders, and upper arms should remain stationary at all times

Single-Joint ❖ Triceps (Back of Upper Arm)

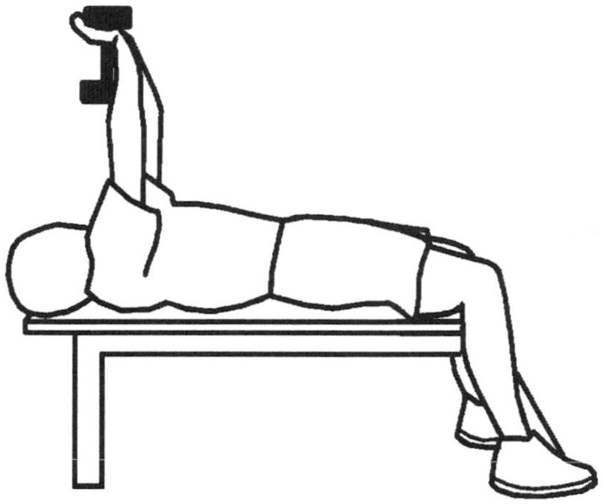

Triceps Extension—Lying Dumbbell

Starting Position

same as for triceps extension—lying EZ curl bar except:

- one end of a dumbbell is cupped with both hands

Finish Position & Movement

same as for triceps extension lying with a barbell except:

- lower the dumbbell until it almost touches the forehead or passes behind the head

Common Technique Errors

Lying EZ Curl Bar and Dumbbell

- moving the shoulders and upper arms to start to lift the weight from the almost-touching-forehead position
- moving the shoulders and upper arms during the lowering or lifting phase

Spotting & Safety

Lying EZ Curl Bar and Dumbbell

- one spotter may stand behind the lifter's head and assist if needed

Muscles Strengthened

Lying EZ Curl Bar and Dumbbell

- back of upper arm (triceps)

Single-Joint ❖ Triceps (Back of Upper Arm)

Triceps Extension—Machine

Starting Position

- sitting on the seat provided
- upper arms resting on the pad provided
- elbows aligned with the center of rotation of the machine's cam
- adjust seat height so that upper arms are parallel to floor
- grasp handles with overhand grip or place hands on pads provided
- elbows are bent as much as possible
- back is straight and feet flat on the floor
- head is upright and looking forward

Finish Position & Movement

- straighten the elbows in a controlled manner until they are completely straight
- return to the starting position in a controlled manner by bending at the elbows
- elbows, shoulders, and upper arms should remain stationary during the entire movement

Common Technique Errors

- using the shoulders, back, or other muscles to assist straightening the elbows
- moving the upper arms and elbows during the movement

Spotting & Safety

- no spotter needed

Muscles Strengthened

- back of upper arm (triceps)

Single-Joint ❖ Triceps (Back of Upper Arm)

Standing Triceps Extension—One-Arm Dumbbell

Variations

EZ Curl Bar

Two-Arm Dumbbell

Starting Position

- using an overhand grip grasp a dumbbell with one hand
- hold the dumbbell overhead with arm fully extended
- place opposite hand on the upper arm to assist in keeping the upper arm still
- stand erect with feet hip width apart
- head is upright and looking forward
- can also be performed seated on a bench

Finish Position & Movement

- bending only at the elbow in a controlled manner, lower dumbbell as far as possible behind the head
- as dumbbell is lowered, palm rotates and faces the side of the head
- moving only at the elbow, return to the starting position in a controlled manner
- elbow, shoulder, and upper arm should remain stationary during the entire movement

Single-Joint ❖ Triceps (Back of Upper Arm)

Standing Triceps Extension—EZ Curl Bar

Starting Position

similar to one-arm dumbbell standing triceps extension except:

- grasp an EZ curl bar in the middle with an overhand grip, hands narrower than shoulder width apart and little finger higher than the thumb when the bar is overhead

Finish Position & Movement

similar to one-arm dumbbell standing triceps extension except:

- in a controlled manner and bending only at the elbows, lower EZ curl bar as far as possible behind the head
- moving only at the elbows, return to the starting position

Single-Joint ❖ Triceps (Back of Upper Arm)

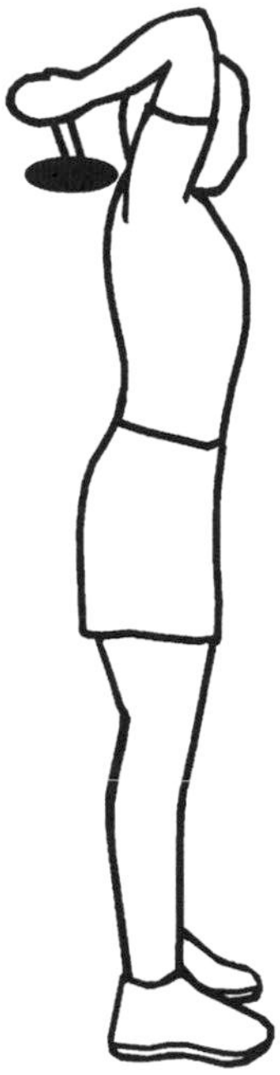

Standing Triceps Extension—Two-Arm Dumbbell

Starting Position

similar to one-arm dumbbell standing triceps extension except:

- grasp a dumbbell by one end with both hands

Finish Position & Movement

similar to one-arm dumbbell standing triceps extension except:

- in a controlled manner and bending only at the elbows, lower dumbbell as far as possible behind the head
- moving only at the elbows return to the starting position

Common Technique Errors

One-Arm Dumbbell, EZ Curl Bar, and Two-Arm Dumbbell

- using the legs, back, or other muscles to lift bar from the behind-the-neck position
- moving the upper arm during the lowering or lifting phase

Spotting & Safety

One-Arm Dumbbell, EZ Curl Bar, and Two-Arm Dumbbell

- one spotter may stand behind the lifter and assist if needed

Muscles Strengthened

One-Arm Dumbbell, EZ Curl Bar, and Two-Arm Dumbbell

- back of upper arm (triceps)

EZ Curl Bar

- trains especially lateral and medial head of triceps

Single-Joint ❖ Triceps (Back of Upper Arm)

Triceps Push-Down—Narrow Grip & Straight Bar

Variation

Rope or Angled Bar

Starting Position

- stand erect, facing the handle of a high pulley or lat pull-down machine
- grasp handle with an overhand grip and palms facing forward and downward
- hands narrower than shoulder width apart
- elbows are completely bent
- upper arms are at the sides
- stand erect with feet hip width apart
- head is upright and looking forward

Finish Position & Movement

- moving only at the elbow, straighten the elbows in a controlled manner until they are completely straight
- moving only at the elbow, return to the starting position in a controlled manner
- elbows, shoulders, and upper arms should remain stationary during the entire movement

Single-Joint ❖ Triceps (Back of Upper Arm)

Triceps Push-Down—Rope or Angled Bar

Starting Position

similar to triceps push-down with a straight bar except:

- using an overhand grip, grasp the rope with palms facing each other or angled bar with little fingers lower than thumb

Finish Position & Movement

similar to triceps push-down with a straight bar except:

- if using a rope, as the elbows straighten spread the hands apart so that, with the elbows straight, the hands are at the sides of the thighs
- if using an angled bar, when the elbows are straight the hands are touching or almost touching the front of the thighs

Common Technique Errors

Straight Bar, Rope, and Angled Bar

- using the shoulder or other muscles to a[illegible] straightening the elbows
- moving the upper arms and elbows during the movement

Spotting & Safety

Straight Bar, Rope, and Angled Bar

- no spotter needed

Muscles Strengthened

Straight Bar, Rope, and Angled Bar

- back of upper arm (triceps)

Rope and Angled Bar

- trains especially lateral and long heads of triceps

Single-Joint ❖ Biceps (Front of Upper Arm)

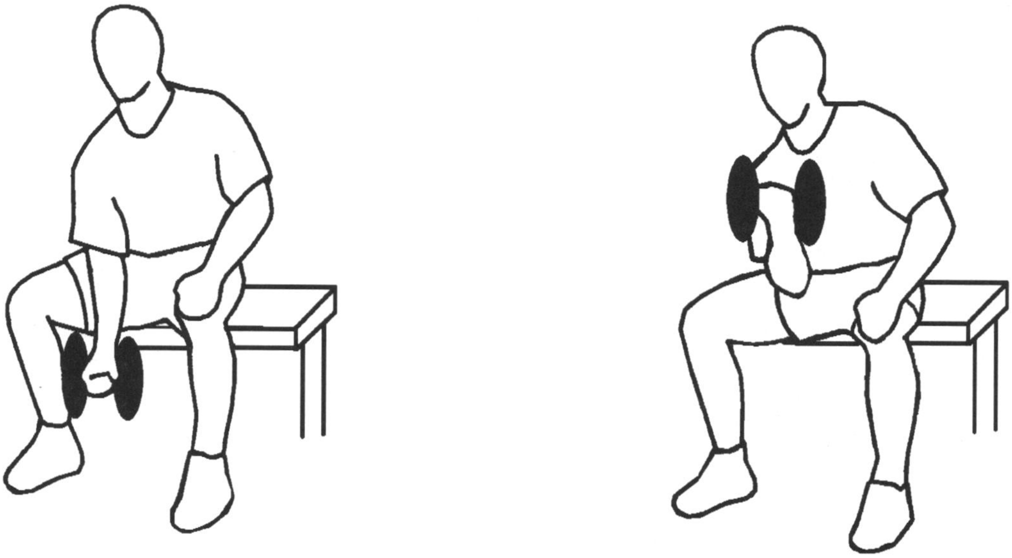

CONCENTRATION CURL

ting Position

- n a flat bench
- asp a dumbbell with an underhand grip and palm facing forward
- the elbow of the arm gasping the dumbbell is straight and resting on the inside of the thigh
- the torso and head are upright
- hand not grasping the dumbbell is resting on the knee on the same side of the body
- feet flat on the floor

Finish Position & Movement

- bending only at the elbow and in a controlled manner, raise the dumbbell until it touches the chest area
- briefly hold the dumbbell in the highest position
- moving only at the elbow, return to the starting position in a controlled manner
- the wrist does not move from the palm-forward position during the movement
- the shoulders, lower back, and head should stay still throughout the entire movement

Common Technique Errors

- using the legs, back, or shoulders to start the lifting movement
- moving the elbow excessively during the exercise

Spotting & Safety

- no spotting is needed
- use of the lower back to start the lifting movement may lead to lower back injury

Muscles Strengthened

- all elbow flexors

Single-Joint ❖ Biceps (Front of Upper Arm)

Incline Seated Dumbbell Arm Curl—Palms Facing Forward

Variation

Palms Facing Thighs—Hammer Curl

Starting Position

- sit on an inclined bench with the back and head flat against the back of the bench
- grasp a dumbbell in each hand with an underhand grip and palms facing forward
- the elbows are straight and down at the sides
- feet flat on the floor

Finish Position & Movement

- moving only at the elbows and in a controlled manner, raise the dumbbells to shoulder height
- keep the palms facing forward throughout the movement
- both dumbbells can be lifted at the same time, or they can be lifted one at a time in an alternating arm fashion
- briefly hold the shoulder-height position
- moving only at the elbows, return to the starting position in a controlled manner
- the shoulders, back, and head should stay still throughout the entire movement

Single-Joint ❖ Biceps (Front of Upper Arm)

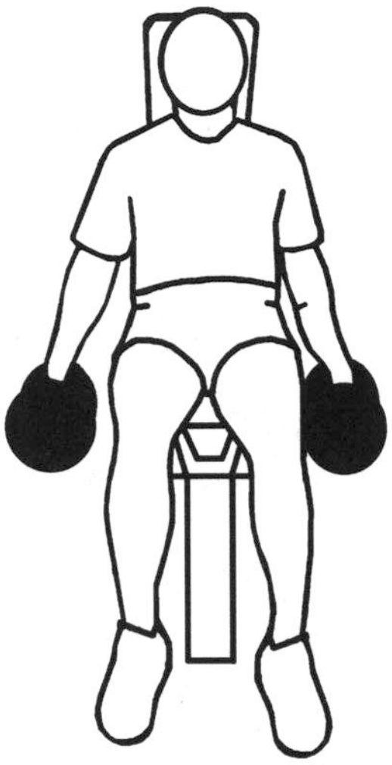

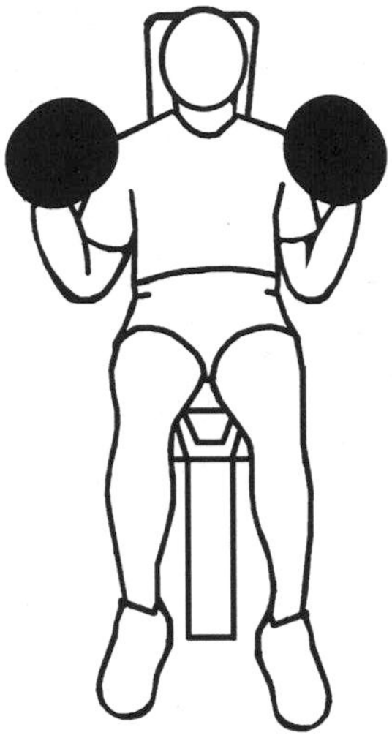

Incline Seated Dumbbell Arm Curl—Palms Facing Thighs—Hammer Curl

Starting Position

similar to incline seated dumbbell arm curl with palms facing forward except:

- grasp a dumbbell in each hand with palms facing the thighs

Finish Position & Movement

similar to incline seated dumbbell arm curl with palms facing forward except:

- keep palms facing thighs (facing each other) throughout the entire movement

Common Technique Errors

Palms Facing Forward and Palms Facing Thighs

- using the back or shoulders to start the lifting movement
- moving the elbows excessively during the exercise

Spotting & Safety

Palms Facing Forward and Palms Facing Thighs

- no spotting is needed

Muscles Strengthened

Palms Facing Forward and Palms Facing Thighs

- all elbow flexors

Palms Facing Forward

- trains especially the medial and lateral heads of biceps

Palms Facing Thighs

- trains especially the lateral head of biceps and brachialis and brachioradialis (located on the thumb side of the forearm)

Single-Joint ❖ Biceps (Front of Upper Arm)

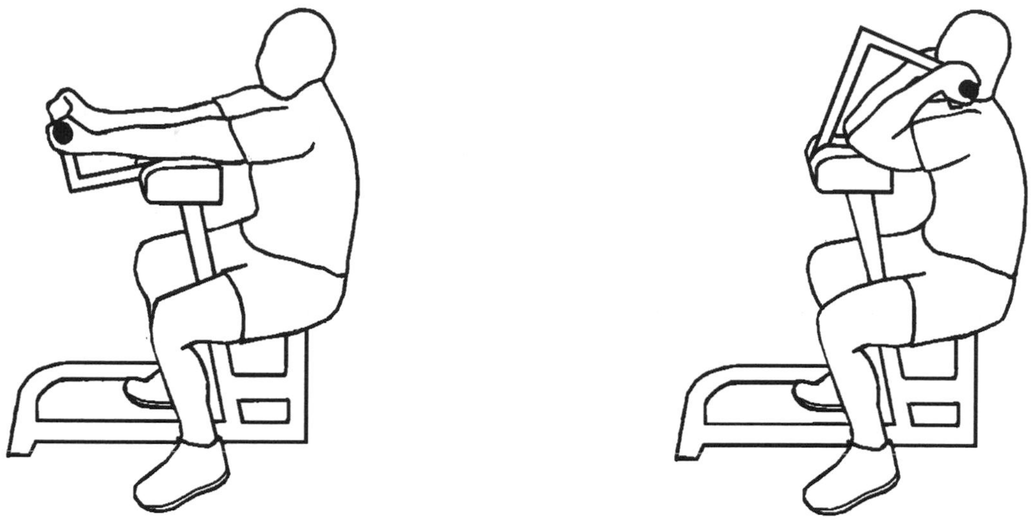

Machine Arm Curl

Starting Position

- sit on the seat
- align elbows with center point of machine's rotation
- adjust seat height so that upper arms are parallel to the floor on some machines and angled to the floor on other machines
- grasp handles with an underhand grip with palms facing upward
- torso is upright and feet flat on the floor
- head is upright and looking forward

Finish Position & Movement

- bending only at the elbows and in a controlled manner, pull the handles upward as far as possible or until they touch the shoulders
- briefly hold this top position
- moving only at the elbows, return to the starting position in a controlled manner
- keep the elbows stationary during the entire movement
- the shoulders, lower back, and head should stay still throughout the entire movement

Common Technique Errors

- using the legs, back, or shoulders to start the lifting movement

Spotting & Safety

- no spotting is needed
- use of the lower back to start the lifting movement may lead to lower back injury

Muscles Strengthened

- all elbow flexors

Single-Joint ❖ Biceps (Front of Upper Arm)

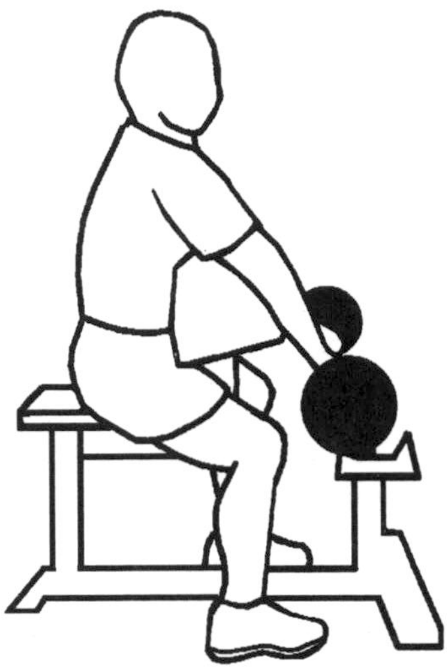

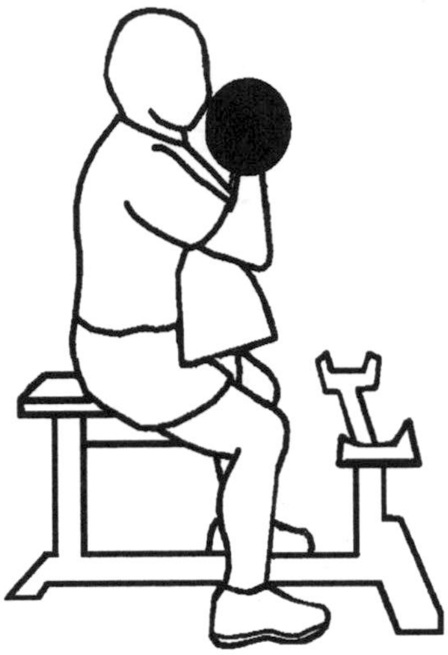

Preacher Bench Curl—Barbell

Variation

EZ Curl Bar

Starting Position

- sit on a preacher curl bench with torso upright and feet flat on the floor
- adjust bench pad height so that it supports the upper arms when sitting upright
- grasp a barbell with an underhand grip with palms facing upward
- hands and elbows are about shoulder width apart
- head is upright and looking forward
- many preacher curl benches have a support from which the bar can be lifted and to which it can be returned after completing the exercise

Finish Position & Movement

- bending only at the elbows and in a controlled manner, raise the bar to shoulder height
- briefly hold the shoulder height position
- moving only at the elbows, return to the starting position in a controlled manner
- do not rest the bar on the supports between reps
- keep the elbows, shoulders, lower back, and head stationary during the entire movement

Single-Joint ❖ Biceps (Front of Upper Arm)

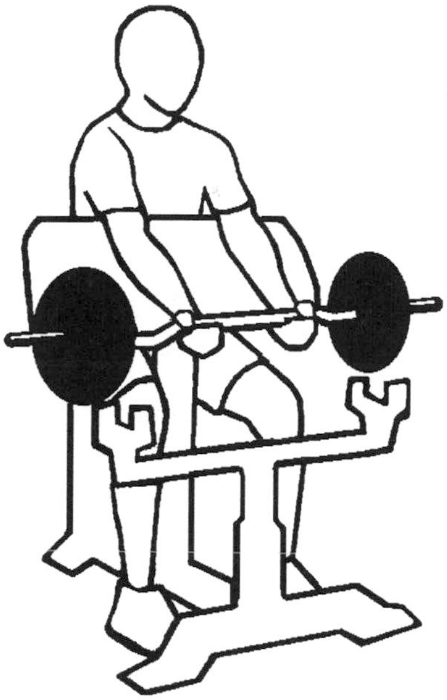

Preacher Bench Curl—EZ Curl Bar

Starting Position

same as for preacher bench curl with a barbell except:

- grasp an EZ curl bar with an underhand grip so that the little finger is lower than the thumb

Finish Position & Movement

same as for preacher bench curl with a barbell

Common Technique Errors

Barbell and EZ Curl Bar

- using the back or shoulders to start the lifting movement
- moving the elbows excessively during the exercise

Spotting & Safety

Barbell and EZ Curl Bar

- one spotter may be used
- the spotter kneels and faces the lifter from the front
- some lifters will not be able to use a straight bar comfortably due to insufficient wrist (supination) flexibility

Muscles Strengthened

Barbell and EZ Curl Bar

- all elbow flexors

Single-Joint ❖ Biceps (Front of Upper Arm)

Standing Arm Curl—Barbell with Wide Grip

Variations

Dumbbells—Palms Facing Forward

Dumbbells—Palms Facing Thighs—Hammer Curl

EZ Curl Bar

Reverse Curl

Starting Position

- grasp a barbell with an underhand grip
- hands are shoulder width or slightly wider apart
- stand erect with the bar resting on the thighs
- feet are hip width apart
- knees are slightly bent
- head is upright and looking forward

Finish Position & Movement

- moving only at the elbows and in a controlled manner, raise the barbell to shoulder height
- briefly hold the shoulder-height position
- moving only at the elbows, return to the starting position in a controlled manner
- keep the elbows close to the body and stationary during the entire movement
- the shoulders, lower back, and head should stay still throughout the entire movement

Single-Joint ❖ Biceps (Front of Upper Arm)

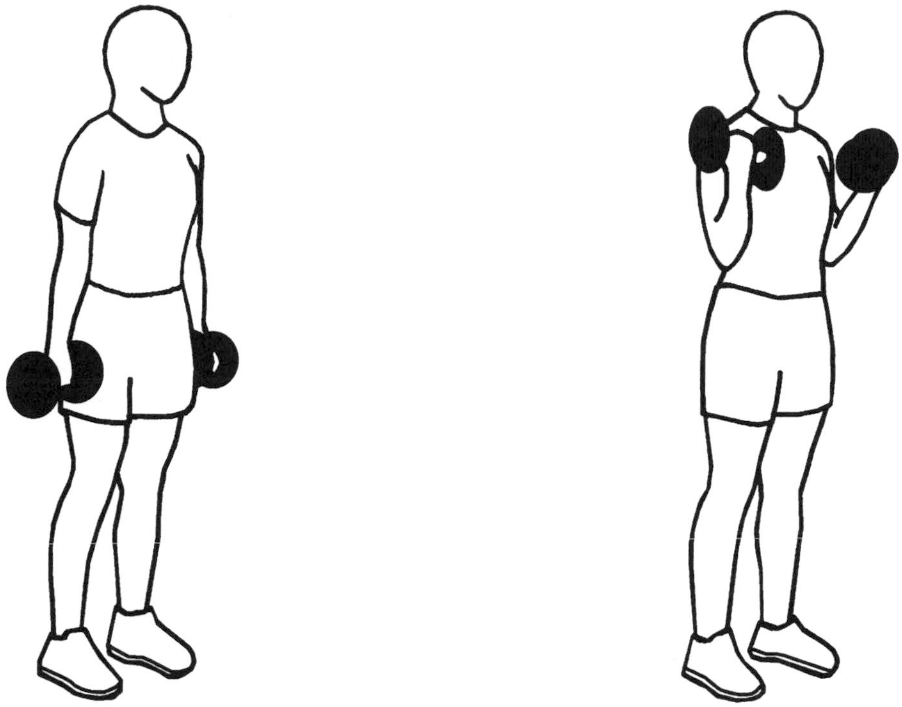

Standing Arm Curl—Dumbbells—Palms Facing Forward

Starting Position

same as for standing arm curl with a barbell and wide grip except:

- grasp a dumbbell with each hand
- use an underhand grip with palms facing forward

Finish Position & Movement

same as for standing arm curl with a barbell and wide grip except:

- moving only at the elbows and in a controlled manner, raise the dumbbells to shoulder height and then lower them back down to the starting position
- keep the palm in forward position during the entire movement
- the dumbbells can be lifted with either both arms at the same time or one arm at a time in an alternating arm action
- briefly hold the shoulder-height position

Single-Joint ❖ Biceps (Front of Upper Arm)

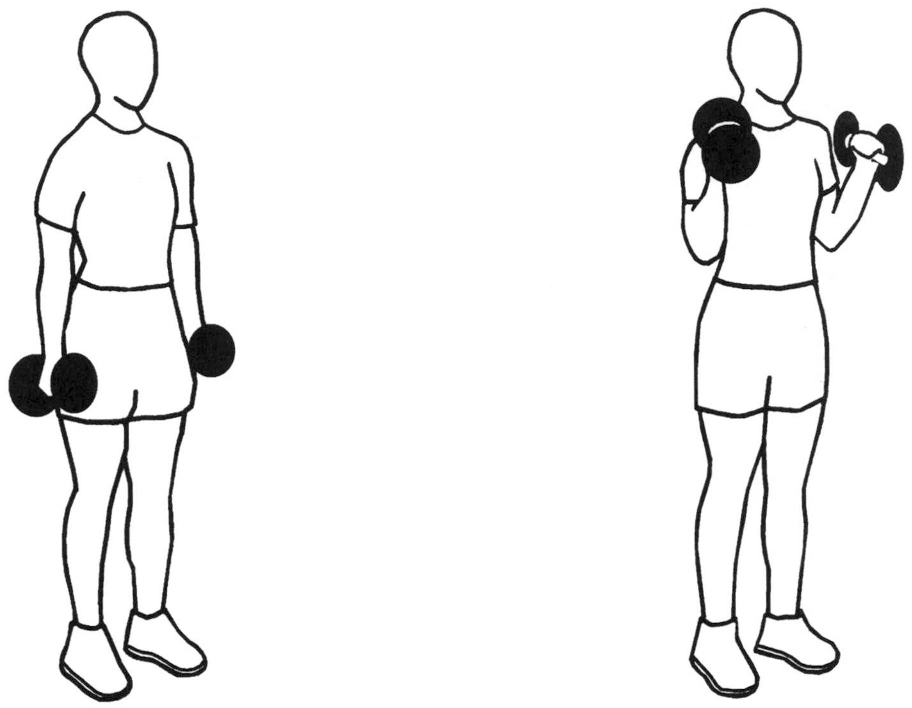

Standing Arm Curl—Dumbbells—Palms Facing Thighs—Hammer Curl

Starting Position

same as for standing arm curl with a barbell and wide grip except:

- grasp a dumbbell with each hand
- use an underhand grip with palms facing the thighs

Finish Position & Movement

same as for standing arm curl with a barbell and wide grip except:

- keep the palms facing the thighs (palms facing each other) throughout the entire movement
- moving only at the elbows and in a controlled manner, raise the dumbbells to shoulder height and then lower them back down to the starting position
- the dumbbells can be lifted with either both arms at the same time or one arm at a time in an alternating arm action

Single-Joint ❖ Biceps (Front of Upper Arm)

Standing Arm Curl—EZ Curl Bar

Starting Position

same as for standing arm curl with a barbell and wide grip except:

- grasp an EZ curl bar with an underhand grip so the thumbs are higher than the little fingers
- hands are shoulder width or slightly wider apart
- stand erect with the EZ curl bar resting on the thighs

Finish Position & Movement

same as for standing arm curl with a barbell and wide grip except:

- moving only at the elbows and in a controlled manner, raise the EZ curl bar to shoulder height and then lower it back down to the starting position

Single-Joint ❖ Biceps (Front of Upper Arm)

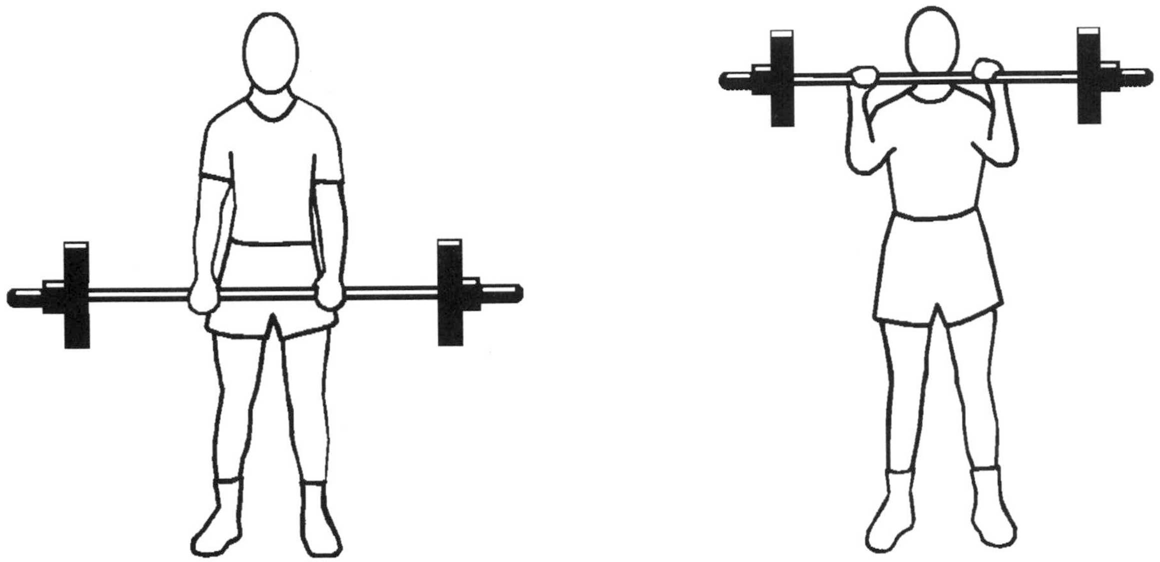

Standing Arm Curl—Reverse Curl

Starting Position

same as for standing arm curl with a barbell and wide grip except:

- grasp a barbell with an overhand grip
- palms are facing the thighs
- hands are shoulder width or slightly wider apart

Finish Position & Movement

same as for standing arm curl with a barbell and wide grip

Common Technique Errors

All Variations of Standing Arm Curl

- using the legs, back, or shoulders to start the lifting movement, which can result in injury
- moving the elbows excessively during the exercise

Spotting & Safety

All Variations of Standing Arm Curl

- no spotting is needed

Barbell with Wide Grip

- some people will not be able to do this exercise comfortably due to insufficient wrist (supination) flexibility

Muscles Strengthened

All Variations of Standing Arm Curl

- all elbow flexors

Barbell with Wide Grip, Dumbbells—Palms Facing Forward, and EZ Curl Bar

- train especially the medial head of biceps

Hammer Curl

- train especially the lateral head of biceps

Hammer Curl and Reverse Curl

- train especially the brachioradialis, a muscle located on the thumb side of the forearm

Single-Joint ❖ Wrist Flexion ❖ Palm Side of Forearm

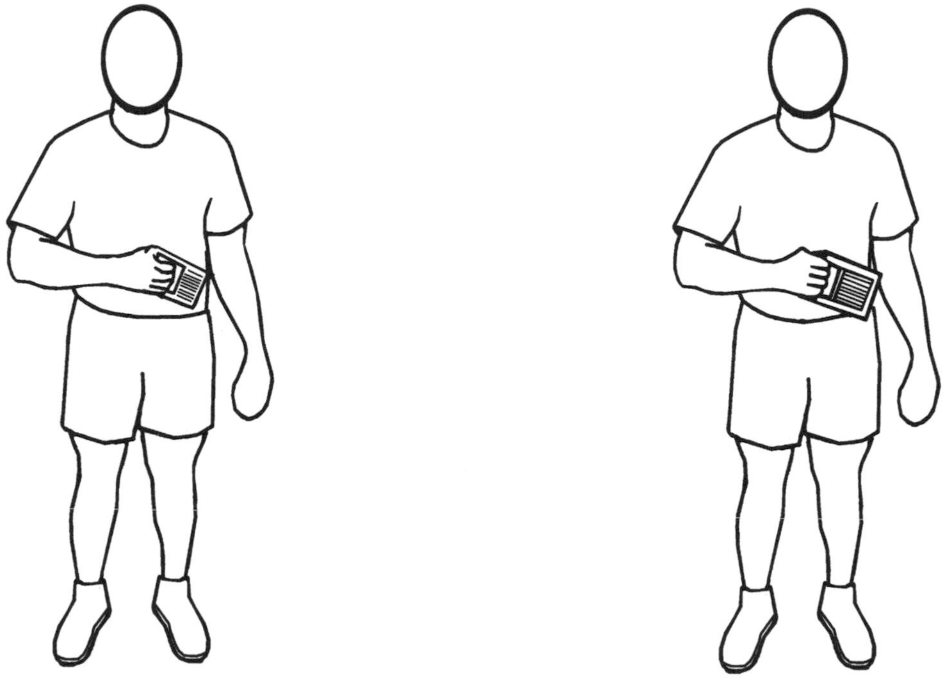

Gripping Exercise

Starting Position

- this exercise requires a tennis ball, portable hand grip exerciser, or stationary machine hand grip exerciser
- if using a tennis ball, hold one in the palm of each hand
- if using a portable hand grip exerciser, grasp the handle in one hand
- if using a stationary machine hand grip exerciser, grasp the handles as instructed by the manufacturer

Finish Position & Movement

- in a controlled manner, squeeze the tennis ball or the machine's handle by flexing the fingers as far as possible
- relax the fingers and repeat gripping for the desired number of repetitions
- change hands if needed after the desired number of repetitions is performed

Common Technique Errors

- on stationary machines, pulling the handles back by pulling with the arms and not just squeezing with the fingers

Spotting & Safety

- no spotter is needed

Muscles Strengthened

- palm side of forearms (finger flexors)

Single-Joint ❖ Wrist Flexion ❖ Palm Side of Forearm

Wrist Curl—Barbell

Variation

Dumbbells

Starting Position

- seated on a bench with feet flat on the floor
- forearms' back of hand side resting completely flat on the thighs
- holding a barbell with both hands with an underhand grip
- palms facing upward and hands about shoulder width apart
- forearms positioned so the wrists are just off of the thighs and free to move up and down
- wrists bent so that the barbell is as high as possible

Finish Position & Movement

- in a controlled manner, lower the barbell toward the floor as far as possible by first bending at the wrist and then extending the fingers
- briefly hold the barbell in the lowest position
- raise the barbell as high as possible by flexing the fingers and then flexing the wrist
- the forearms should remain still and in contact with the thighs at all times
- the back and head should stay upright and the feet should stay flat on the floor at all times

Single-Joint ❖ Wrist Flexion ❖ Palm Side of Forearm

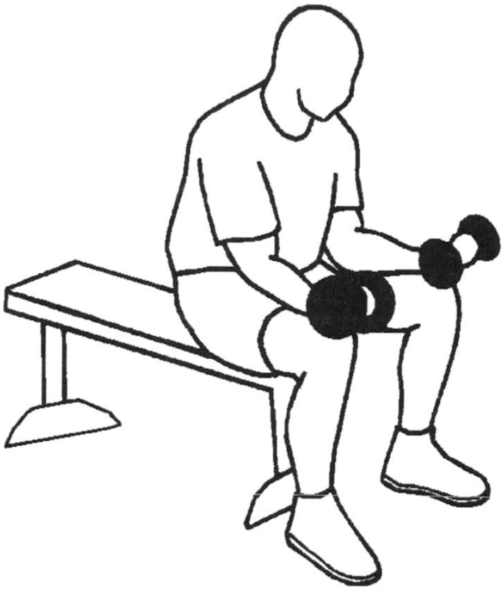

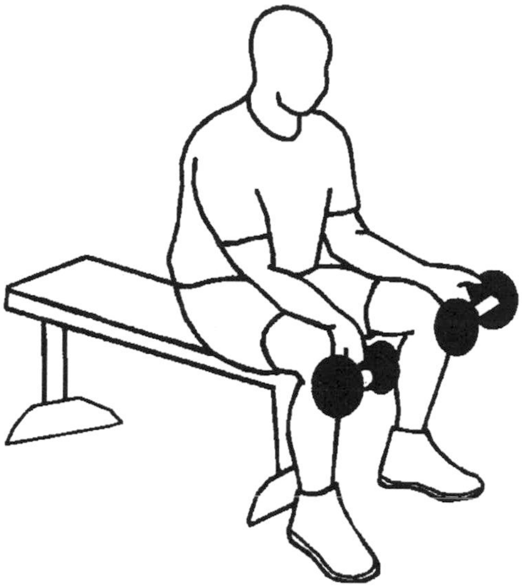

Wrist Curl—Dumbbells

Starting Position

similar to wrist curl with a barbell except:

- ♦ holding dumbbells in each hand with an underhand grip

Finish Position & Movement

similar to wrist curl with a barbell except:

- ♦ in a controlled manner lower both dumbbells toward the floor as far as possible and then raise both dumbbells as high as possible

Common Technique Errors

Barbell and Dumbbells

- ♦ rising up on the toes to help lift the barbell or dumbbells from the lowest position
- ♦ moving the forearms to help lift the barbell or dumbbells

Spotting & Safety

Barbell and Dumbbells

- ♦ no spotter is needed

Muscles Strengthened

Barbell and Dumbbells

- ♦ entire palm side of forearm (wrist flexors)

Single-Joint ❖ Wrist Extension ❖ Backhand Side of Forearm

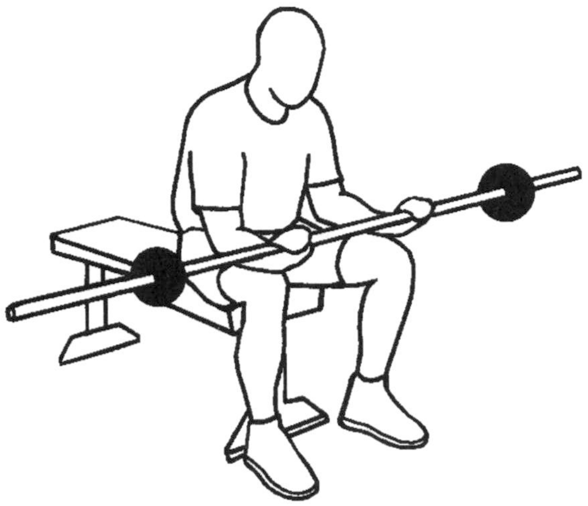

Reverse Wrist Curl—Barbell

Variation

Dumbbells

Starting Position

- seated on a bench with feet flat on the floor
- palm side of forearms resting completely flat on the thighs
- a barbell is held with an overhand grip
- palms are facing downward and hands are about shoulder width apart
- forearms positioned so that the wrists are just off of the thighs and free to move
- wrists bent so that the barbell is as high as possible

Finish Position & Movement

- in a controlled manner, lower the barbell toward the floor as far as possible by bending at the wrist
- briefly hold the barbell in the lowest position
- raise the barbell in a controlled manner as high as possible by extending the wrist
- the forearms should remain still and in contact with the thighs at all times
- the back and head should stay upright and the feet should stay flat on the floor at all times

Single-Joint ❖ Wrist Extension ❖ Backhand Side of Forearm

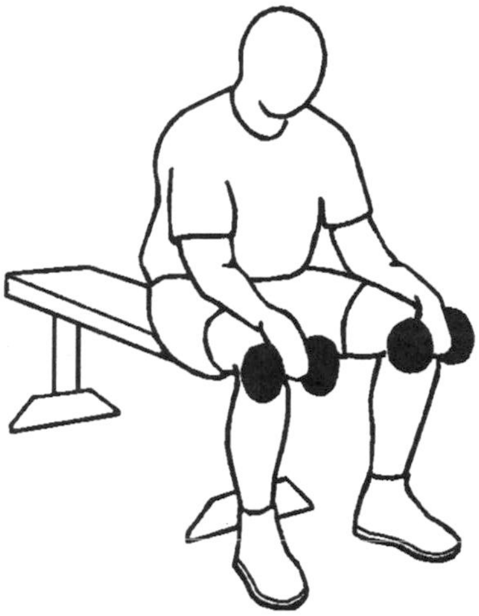

Reverse Wrist Curl—Dumbbells

Starting Position

same as for reverse wrist curl with a barbell except:

- a dumbbell is held in both hands with an overhand grip

Finish Position & Movement

similar to reverse wrist curl with a barbell except:

- in a controlled manner, lower both dumbbells toward the floor as far as possible and then raise both dumbbells as high as possible by bending at the wrist

Common Technique Errors

Barbell and Dumbbells

- rising up on the toes to help lift the barbell or dumbbells from the lowest position
- moving the forearms to help lift the barbell or dumbbells

Spotting & Safety

Barbell and Dumbbells

- no spotter is needed

Muscles Strengthened

Barbell and Dumbbells

- entire backhand side of forearm (wrist extensors)

Single-Joint ❖ Wrist Flexion and Extension ❖ Both Sides of Forearm

Wrist Roller—Wooden Handle

Variation

Machine

Starting Position

- standing with feet hip width apart
- grasping the wooden handle with an overhand grip and palms facing downward
- torso and head upright
- upper arms are at the sides
- elbows at a 90 degree angle and forearms parallel to the floor

Finish Position & Movement

- in a controlled manner, alternately move the wrists to wrap the cord around the wooden handle
- clockwise rotation trains the wrist extensors located on the forearms' backhand sides
- counterclockwise rotation trains the wrist flexors located on the forearms' palm sides
- after the cord is completely wrapped on the wooden handle, unwrap it by alternately moving the wrists
- the forearms should stay parallel to the floor at all times
- the back and head should stay upright and the feet should stay flat on the floor at all times

Single-Joint ❖ Wrist Flexion and Extension ❖ Both Sides of Forearm

Wrist Roller—Machine

Starting Position

similar to wrist roller with a wooden handle except:

- standing with feet hip width apart or seated, depending on the machine
- grasp the round handle with an overhand grip and palms facing downward

Finish Position & Movement

same as for wrist roller with a wooden handle

Common Technique Errors

Wooden Handle and Machine

- moving the forearms to help roll the wrists

Spotting & Safety

Wooden Handle and Machine

- no spotter is needed

Muscles Strengthened

Wooden Handle and Machine

- clockwise rotation trains the wrist extensors located on the forearms' backhand sides
- counterclockwise rotation trains the wrist flexors located on the forearms' palm sides

Multi-Joint ❖ Lower Body

Back Squat—Barbell

Variation

Dumbbell Squat

Starting Position

- standing, feet hip width or slightly wider apart
- feet flat on the floor
- toes pointing straight forward or slightly to the side
- back straight and head upright
- barbell resting on the spines of the shoulder blades
- hands grasping barbell wider than shoulder width
- palms facing forward and thumbs wrapped around the barbell
- body weight on the mid-foot and heels
- barbell should be removed from a power rack or squat rack to get into the starting position

Finish Position & Movement

- in a controlled manner, bend at the knees and hips until the top of the thighs are parallel to floor
- the knees should move forward in line with the toes as you bend
- in a controlled manner, return to starting position
- there will be some forward lean, but stay as upright as possible
- the feet should remain flat on the floor
- body weight stays on mid-foot and heels throughout the motion
- head stays upright and does not tilt back to look at the ceiling
- shoulders stay back throughout entire motion
- knees should not be out in front of toes at any time during the motion

Multi-Joint ❖ Lower Body

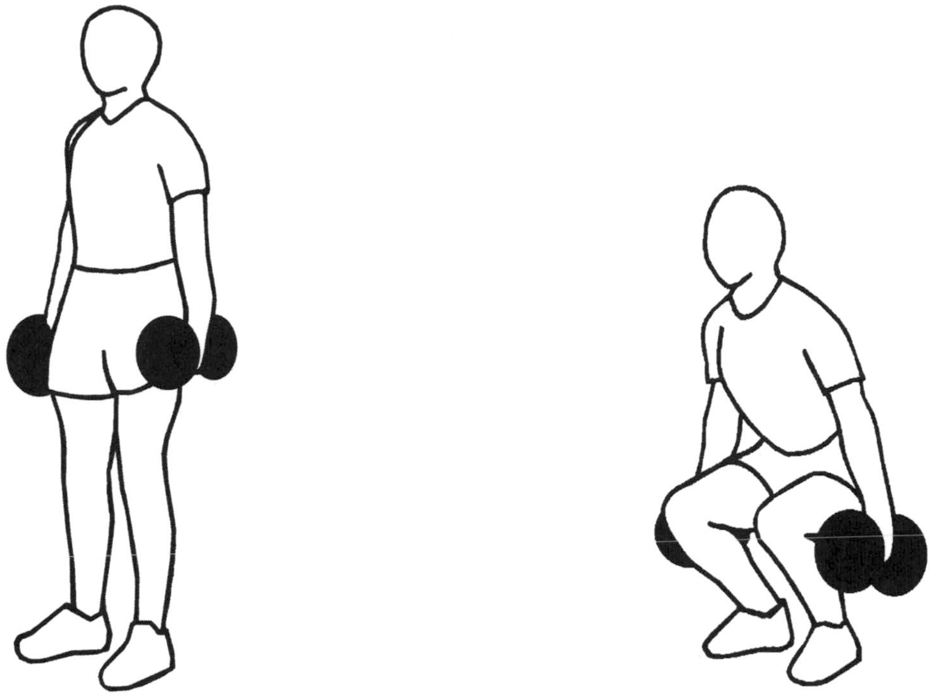

Dumbbell Squat

Starting Position

similar to back squat with a barbell except:

- a dumbbell is held in each hand
- arms are at the sides

Finish Position & Movement

similar to back squat with a barbell except:

- the dumbbells remain at arm's length at the sides throughout the exercise movement

Common Technique Errors

Barbell and Dumbbells

- too much forward lean places stress on lower back
- tall people will have trouble squatting correctly because of their long legs and back
- not keeping feet flat on floor—a solid 1- to 2-inch high nonslip object may be placed under the heels to help this problem
- strengthening abdominals and lower back will help with correct technique

Spotting & Safety

Barbell

- use two spotters (one at each end of the bar)
- barbell squats should be done in a power rack

Dumbbells

- the dumbbell squat is easier to do with the back upright and so causes less lower back strain

Muscles Strengthened

Barbell and Dumbbells

- entire leg and hip area
- buttocks (gluteals), back of thigh (hamstrings), front of thigh (quadriceps), and lower back (spinal erectors)

Multi-Joint ❖ Lower Body

Dead Lift—Barbell

Variations

Dumbbells

Smith Machine

Starting Position

- standing with the feet hip width or slightly wider apart
- feet flat on the floor and toes pointing straight forward or slightly to the side
- bar above the point where toes meet the foot
- knees and hips bent just far enough to grasp the barbell
- back is straight and head upright
- shoulders are directly above or slightly in front of the bar and the elbows are straight
- hands grasping barbell slightly wider than shoulder width apart
- either two overhand grips (palms facing backward) or a mixed grip, one overhand and one underhand (palm facing forward), can be used
- thumbs are wrapped around the barbell
- body weight is on the mid-foot and heels

Finish Position & Movement

- lift the bar to knee height by only straightening the knees
- do not straighten the back or hips to lift the bar to knee height
- the angle of the back to the floor should stay the same until bar is past the knees
- once the bar is past the knees, the hips start to straighten and the back becomes more upright
- straighten hips, knees, and back until bar is resting on thighs with the shoulders back

- in a controlled manner, return to starting position
- do not look up at the ceiling; the head stays in line with the rest of the back
- body weight is over the mid-foot and rear foot for the entire motion
- elbows are straight for the entire motion

Multi-Joint ❖ Lower Body

Dead Lift—Dumbbells

Starting Position

similar to dead lift with a barbell except:

- an overhand grip is used with palms facing the thighs to grasp a dumbbell in each hand

Finish Position & Movement

similar to dead lift with a barbell

Multi-Joint ❖ Lower Body

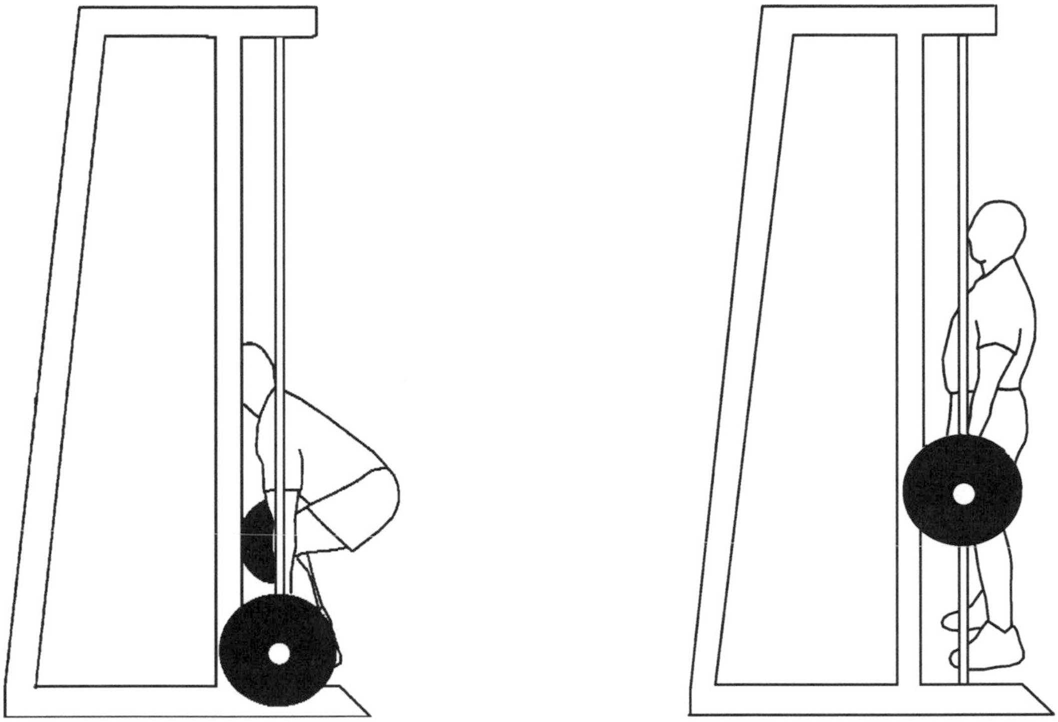

Dead Lift—Smith Machine

Starting Position

same as for dead lift with a barbell except:

- the lower stops of the machine can be adjusted to the approximate height of a barbell with 45-pound plates on it

Finish Position & Movement

similar to dead lift with a barbell except:

- the bar will not move forward or back, so the path of the bar when lifting and lowering will be in a perfectly straight line

Common Technique Errors

Barbell, Dumbbells, and Smith Machine

- shoulders behind the bar in starting position
- not having feet flat on the floor in starting position
- having weight over the toes and not on mid-foot and heels in starting position
- strengthening abdominals and lower back will help with correct technique
- not lowering the bar in a controlled manner but bouncing the weights off of the floor to start the next repetition

Spotting & Safety

Barbell, Dumbbells, and Smith Machine

- no spotters are needed

Barbell

- bumper plates should be used if available

Muscles Strengthened

Barbell, Dumbbells, and Smith Machine

- entire leg, hip, and back areas
- buttocks (gluteals), back of thigh (hamstrings), front of thigh (quadriceps), and lower back (spinal erectors)

Multi-Joint ❖ Lower Body

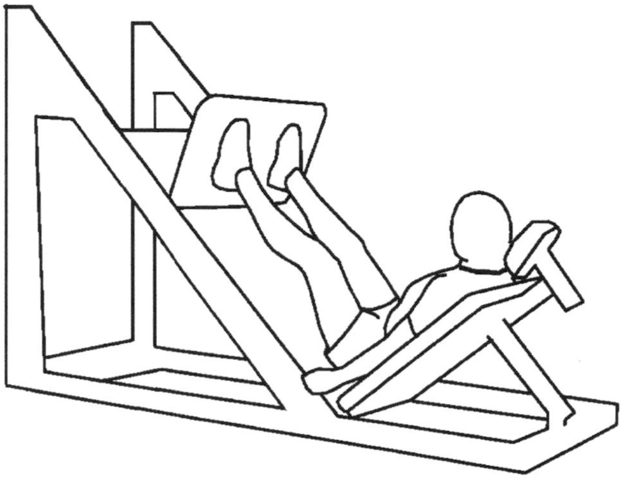

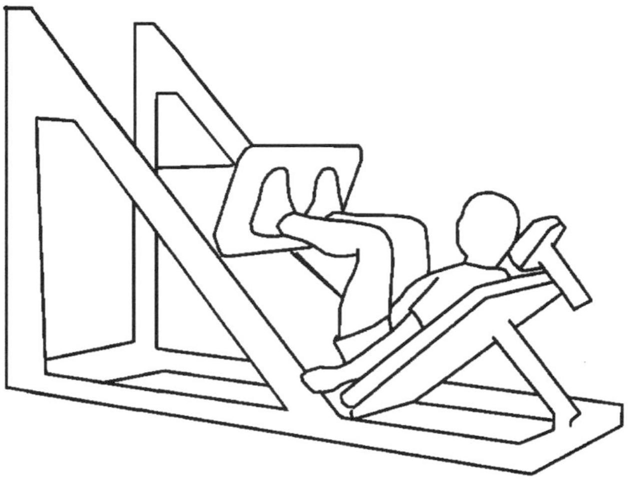

Hip Sled

Starting Position

- lying on the back, entire back and shoulders in contact with the back pad
- if possible adjust stops so that the sled stops moving downward right before the hips begin to rotate upward
- feet flat on the foot platform and slightly wider than hip width apart
- straighten legs and swivel handles located on the sides of the machine so that the sled can move downward
- if provided, grasp handles near hips
- weight is adjusted by placing weight plates on pegs on the sides of the sled or moving part of the machine

Finish Position & Movement

- in a controlled manner, bend legs until just before the hips begin to rotate upward
- in a controlled manner, straighten the legs until the knees are straight
- straighten but do not lock the knees
- the entire back maintains contact with the back pad throughout the motion
- feet remain flat on the foot platform at all times
- after completion of a set, swivel handles near the hips so that the sled rests on stops and can not come downward

Common Technique Errors

- lowering the sled too far so that the hips and lower back come off the back pad, which can result in lower back injury

Spotting & Safety

- no spotting needed
- if provided, make sure stops are adjusted so that the sled cannot pin you in the lowest position

Muscles Strengthened

- entire leg and hip area
- buttocks (gluteals), front of thigh (quadriceps), back of thigh (hamstrings), inside of thigh (hip abductors)

Multi-Joint ❖ Lower Body

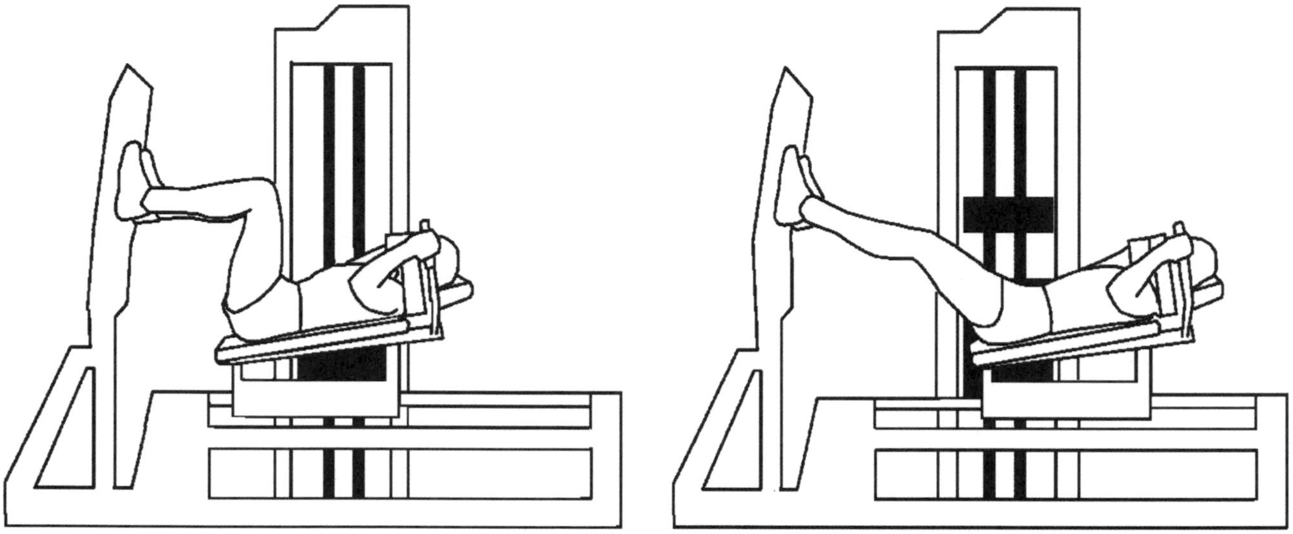

Leg Press

Starting Position

- lying on the back, entire back and shoulders in contact with the back pad
- shoulders are in contact with the shoulder pads
- feet are flat on the foot platform
- adjust the distance the back pad is from the foot platform so that a 90 degree knee angle is achieved in the starting position
- if provided, grasp handles
- on some machines a high or low foot placement on the platform may be used
- a high foot placement emphasizes the hamstrings more than a low foot placement does
- a low foot placement emphasizes the quadriceps more than a high foot placement does

Finish Position & Movement

- in a controlled manner, straighten the legs
- straighten the knees but do not lock them
- hold the legs in the straight position briefly and, in a controlled manner, return to the starting position
- the entire back maintains contact with the back pad throughout the motion
- the shoulders maintain contact with the shoulder pads at all times
- feet remain flat on the foot platform at all times

Common Technique Errors

- bouncing weights out of starting position after completion of a repetition to assist with the next repetition

- not keeping feet flat on the foot platform
- not starting from a 90 degree knee angle

Spotting & Safety

- no spotting needed
- not keeping the back flat on the back pad may result in back injury

Muscles Strengthened

- entire leg and hip area
- buttocks (gluteals), front of thigh (quadriceps), back of thigh (hamstrings), inside of thigh (hip adductors)

Multi-Joint ❖ Lower Body

Lunge—Barbell

Variation

Dumbbells

Starting Position

- standing, feet hip width apart
- feet flat on the floor
- back straight and head upright
- barbell resting on the spines of the shoulder blades
- hands grasping barbell wider than shoulder width apart with an overhand grip and thumbs wrapped around the barbell
- barbell should be removed from a power rack or squat rack to get into the starting position

Finish Position & Movement

- in a controlled manner, step straight forward with one leg so that the feet are still hip width apart after the step
- the step is long enough so that when in the finish position, the knee is above the mid-foot and not in front or behind the toes
- in a controlled manner, bend the knee of the front leg until the knee of the rear leg almost touches the floor
- the front foot remains flat on the floor
- the rear foot can rise up onto the toes when the front leg is bent
- after bending the front leg, straighten it completely but do not lock it, then repeat the bending of the front leg
- after the desired number of repetitions, push off of the floor with the front leg and in two short steps return to the starting position
- the torso remains upright throughout the motion
- repeat with the opposite leg
- a variation is to return to the starting standing position (feet hip width apart) after each bending of the front leg

Multi-Joint ❖ Lower Body

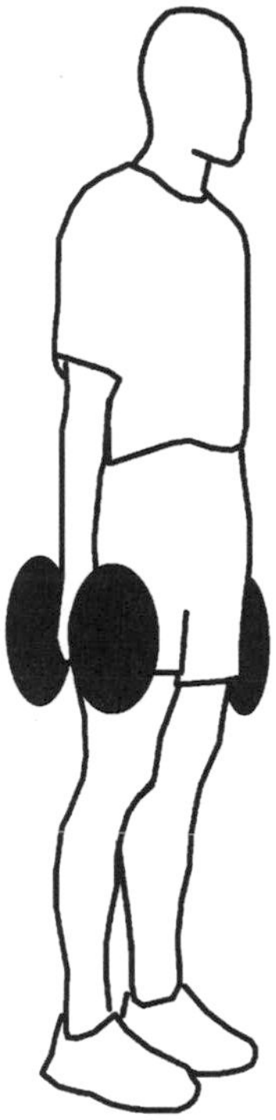

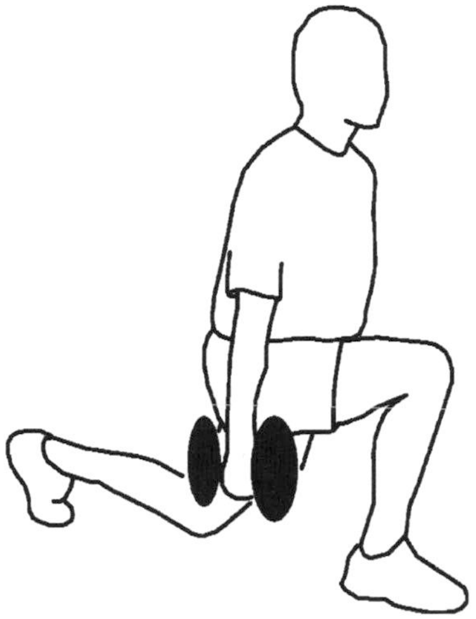

Lunge—Dumbbells

Starting Position

similar to lunge with a barbell except:

- a dumbbell is held in each hand with an overhand grip
- arms hanging straight down at the sides
- palms facing the thighs

Finish Position & Movement

similar to lunge with a barbell except:

- the dumbbells remain hanging straight down at the sides throughout the entire exercise motion

Common Technique Errors

Barbell and Dumbbells

- a step which is too short so that the front knee is in front of the toes when the leg is bent
- a step which is too long so that the front knee is behind the heel when the leg is bent
- not keeping the torso upright places stress on the lower back
- not stepping straight forward, which results in the feet not being hip width apart after the step; this causes difficulty in maintaining balance because of a narrow base of support

Spotting & Safety

Barbell and Dumbbells

- a step forward that is not of the correct length places undue stress on the knee

Barbell

- two spotters (one at each end of the bar) can be used

Dumbbells

- no spotters are needed
- dumbbell lunges are easier to perform than barbell lunges because it is easier to keep the torso upright when doing the former

Muscles Strengthened

Barbell and Dumbbells

- entire leg and hip area of the front leg
- buttocks (gluteals), back of thigh (hamstrings), front of thigh (quadriceps)

Single-Joint ❖ Quadriceps (Front of Thigh)

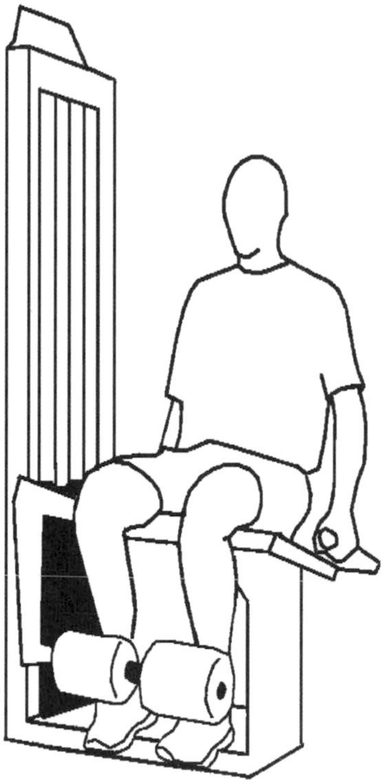

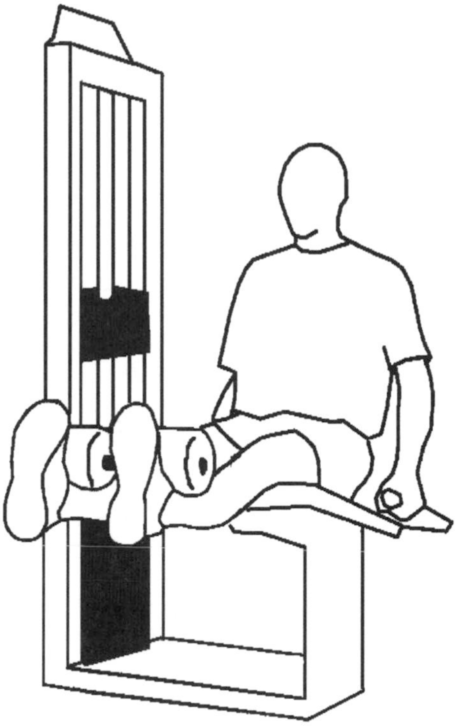

Knee Extension—Toes Pointing Straight Forward

Variations

Toes Pointing In

Toes Pointing Out

Starting Position

- sitting on the seat provided
- back flat against the back of seat
- front of ankles hooked under the pads provided
- toes pointing straight forward when knees are bent to a 90 degree angle
- adjust the machine so that the ankle pad is just above the ankles and allows the toes to be pulled up
- if possible, adjust the range-of-motion limiter to allow for a full knee extension and a 90 degree knee angle when knees are bent
- center of knee is in line with the center of rotation of the machine; if possible, adjust the machine for this
- grasp the handles near hips if provided

Finish Position & Movement

- keeping the back against the seat, in a controlled manner, straighten the knees
- straighten the knees completely, but do not lock them
- hold the highest position briefly, and return to the starting position in a controlled manner
- keep the toes pointing straight forward at all times

Single-Joint ❖ Quadriceps (Front of Thigh)

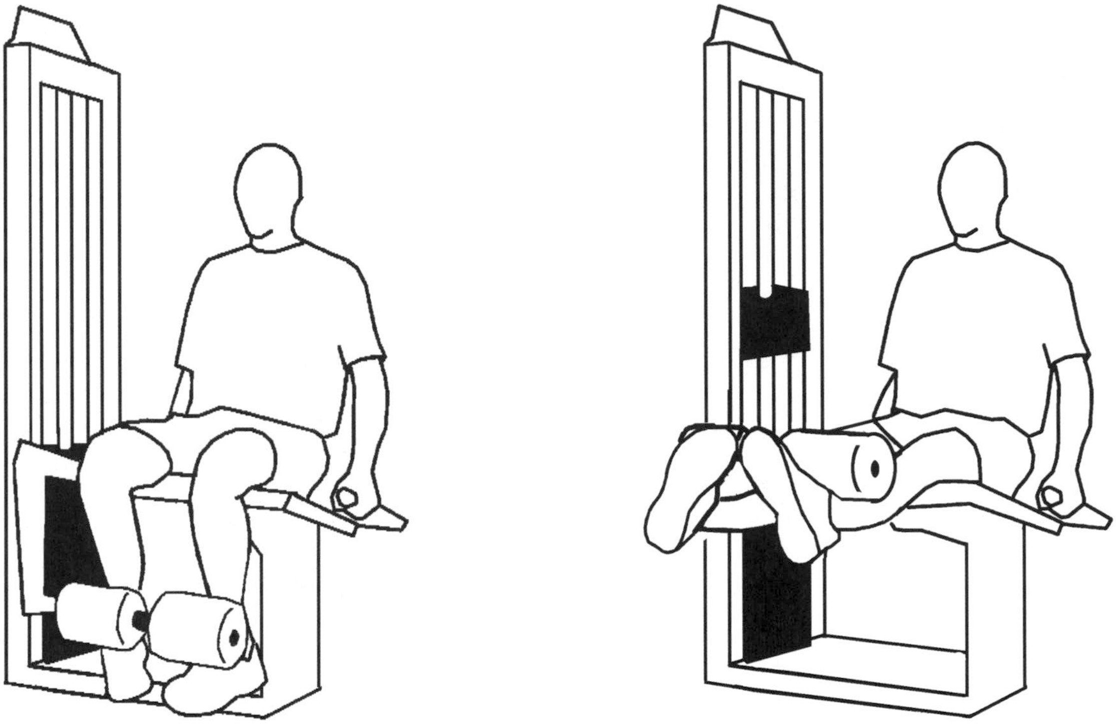

Knee Extension—Toes Pointing In

Starting Position

same as for knee extension with the toes pointing straight forward except:

- toes are pointing in when in the starting position

Finish Position & Movement

same as for knee extension with the toes pointing straight forward except:

- keep toes pointing in at all times

Single-Joint ❖ Quadriceps (Front of Thigh)

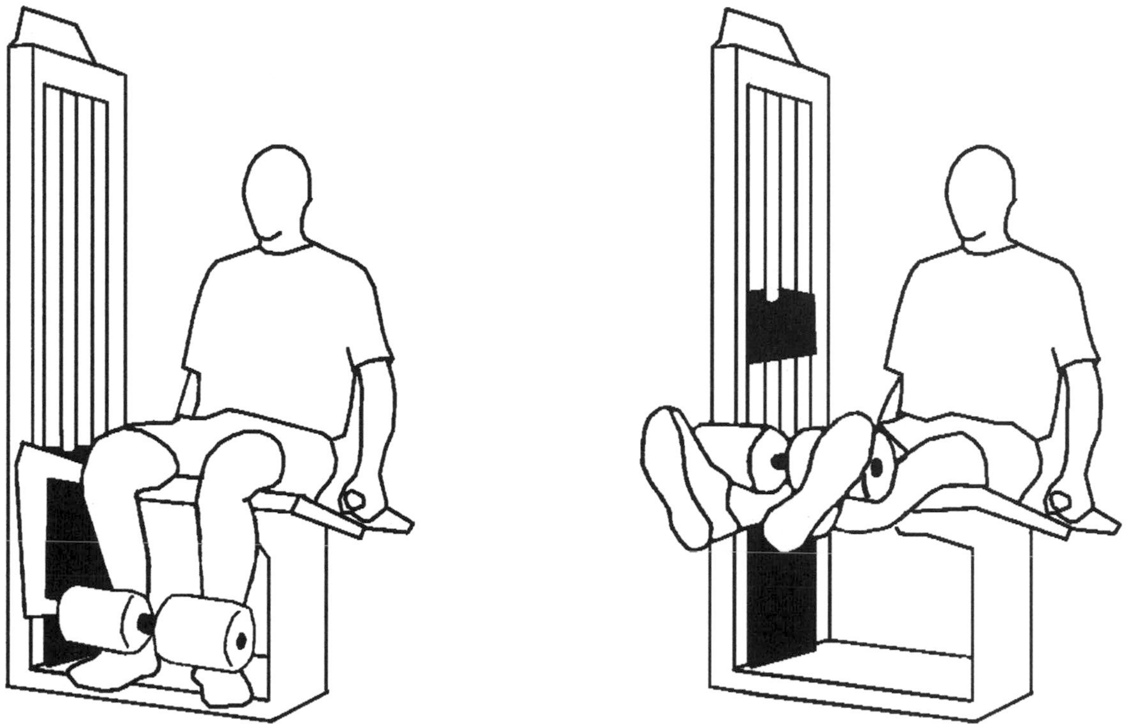

KNEE EXTENSION—TOES POINTING OUT

Starting Position

same as for knee extension with the toes pointing straight forward except:

- toes are pointing out when in the starting position

Finish Position & Movement

same as for knee extension with the toes pointing straight forward except:

- keep toes pointing out at all times

Common Technique Errors

Toes Pointing Straight Forward, Toes Pointing In, and Toes Pointing Out

- rocking the hips to help start the movement
- jerking with the lower back to start the movement may cause lower back injury

Spotting & Safety

Toes Pointing Straight Forward, Toes Pointing In, and Toes Pointing Out

- no spotting is needed

Muscles Strengthened

Toes Pointing Straight Forward, Toes Pointing In, and Toes Pointing Out

- front of thigh (quadriceps)

Toes Pointing In

- front of the thigh but especially the outside (vastus lateralis) and middle (vastus intermedius) portions of the quadriceps

Toes Pointing Out

- front of thigh but especially the lower inside (vastus medialis) and middle (vastus intermedius) portions of the quadriceps and rectus femoris

Single-Joint ❖ Hamstrings (Back of Thigh)

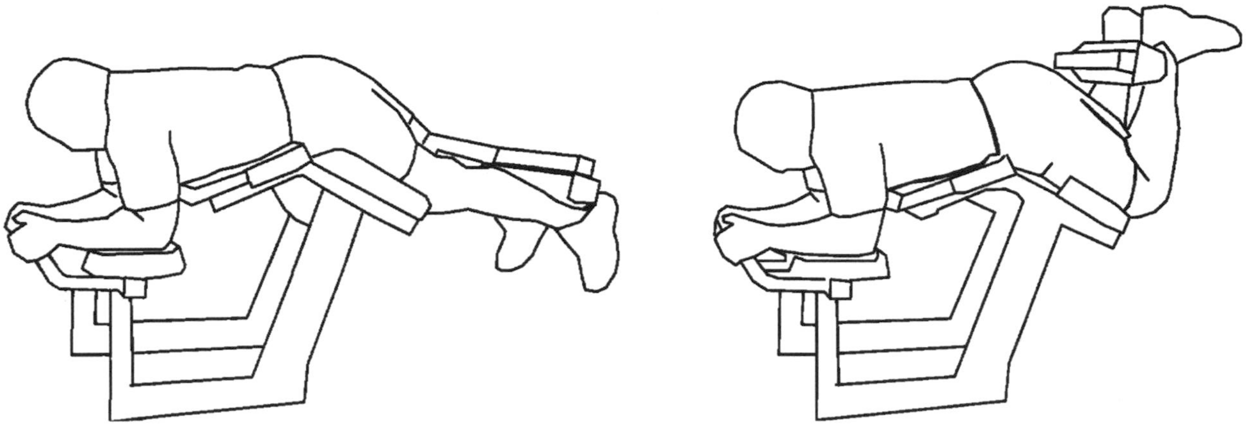

Knee Curl—Lying

Variations

Seated

Standing

Starting Position

- lying on the stomach on the bench provided
- back of the ankles hooked under the pads provided
- adjust the machine so that the ankle pad is just above the heel
- grasp the handles provided
- if possible, adjust the range-of-motion limiter to allow for a full knee extension and for heels to touch the buttocks when in the finish position
- center of the knee is in line with the center of rotation of the machine

Finish Position & Movement

- in a controlled manner and keeping the stomach and hips flat against the bench, bend the knees
- bend the knees until the ankle pads touch the buttocks or stops
- briefly hold the ankle pads against the buttocks or stops, and return to the starting position in a controlled manner

Single-Joint ❖ Hamstrings (Back of Thigh)

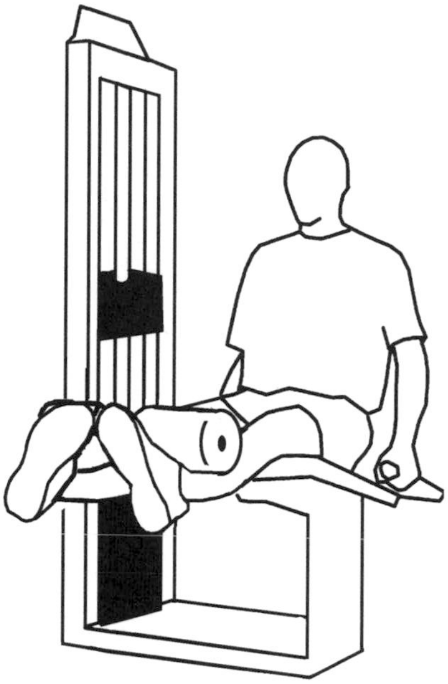

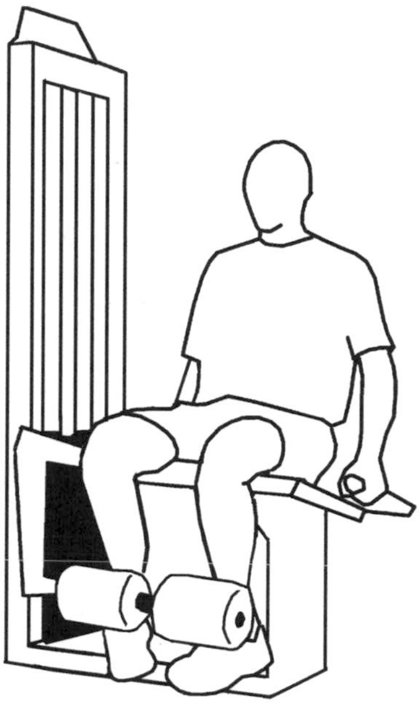

Knee Curl—Seated

Starting Position

- ♦ sit on the seat provided
- ♦ back of ankles hooked over the pads provided
- ♦ adjust the machine so that the ankle pad is just above the heel
- ♦ grasp the handles provided
- ♦ if possible, adjust the range-of-motion limiter to allow for a full knee extension and a knee angle of 90 degrees or less when knees are bent
- ♦ center of the knee is in line with the center of rotation of the machine
- ♦ adjust the height of the pad that rests on top of the thighs, if provided

Finish Position & Movement

- ♦ keeping the buttocks and back against the bench, in a controlled manner, bend the knees
- ♦ bend the knees as far as possible
- ♦ briefly hold the greatest knee-bend position, and return to the starting position in a controlled manner

Single-Joint ❖ Hamstrings (Back of Thigh)

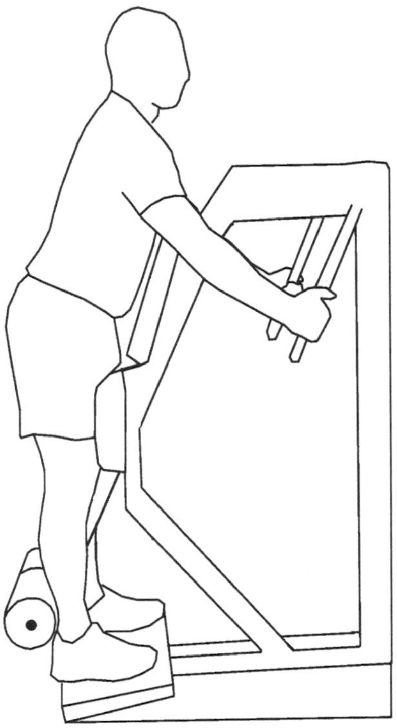

Knee Curl—Standing

Starting Position

- standing predominantly on one foot
- ankle pad just above the heels
- thigh pads above the knees
- adjust the height of the ankle and thigh pads if possible
- grasp the handles provided
- center of the knee is in line with the center of rotation of the machine; if possible, adjust the machine to accomplish this

Finish Position & Movement

- bend the knee of one leg while standing on the other leg
- bend the knee until the ankle pad touches the buttocks or as far as possible
- briefly hold the highest ankle position, and return to the starting position in a controlled manner
- perform the desired number of repetitions and switch legs

Common Technique Errors

Lying, Seated, and Standing

- rocking the hips to help start the movement
- jerking with the lower back to start the movement
- not touching the buttocks or stops with the ankle pads

Spotting & Safety

Lying, Seated, and Standing

- no spotting is needed

- jerking with the lower back to start the exercise movement may result in lower back injury

Muscles Strengthened

Lying, Seated, and Standing

- back of thigh (hamstrings)

Lying

- trains especially the middle (semitendinosus) and outer (biceps femoris) portions of the hamstrings

Seated

- trains especially the middle (semitendinosus) portion of the hamstrings

Single-Joint ❖ Hip Abduction

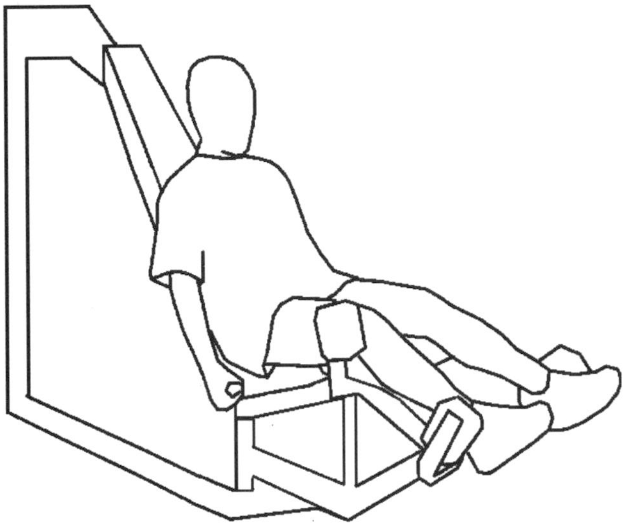

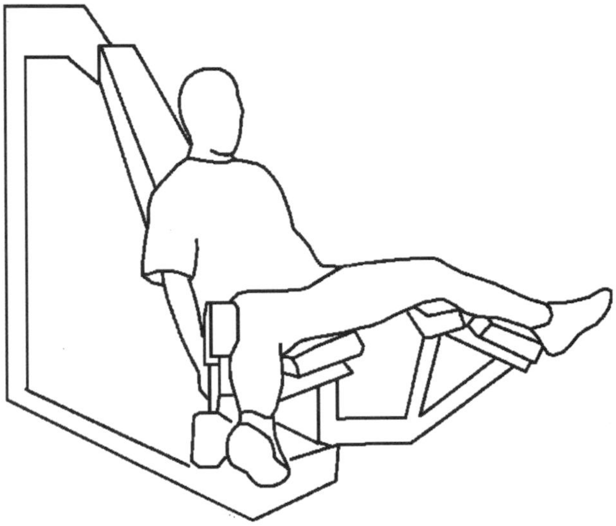

Hip Abduction—Machine

Starting Position

- seated on the seat provided
- head, lower back, and upper back in contact with the seat back
- legs close together
- leg pads on the outside of the leg above the knee
- toes pointing straight up
- hands grasping the handles if provided

Finish Position & Movement

- in a controlled manner, spread the legs as far as possible
- hold the widest position briefly
- in a controlled manner, return to the starting position
- toes remain pointing straight up at all times
- head, lower back, and upper back maintain contact with the seat back at all times

Common Technique Errors

- rocking the hips and lower back to help start the movement
- not spreading the legs as far as possible

Spotting & Safety

- no spotting is needed

Muscles Strengthened

- outer thigh and buttocks (hip abductors)

Single-Joint ❖ Hip Abduction

Hip Abduction—Lying

Starting Position

- lying on the side on the floor
- upper body supported by the arm nearest the floor
- legs together
- toes pointing forward
- resistance can be added by attaching an ankle weight just above the knee

Finish Position & Movement

- in a controlled manner, raise the top leg as far as possible
- toes remain pointing forward at all times
- hold the highest position briefly
- in a controlled manner, return to the starting position
- head, lower back, and upper back remain still at all times
- after completing the desired number of repetitions, switch legs

Common Technique Errors

- rocking the hips and lower back to help start the movement
- not spreading the legs as far as possible
- not keeping the toes pointing forward

Spotting & Safety

- no spotting is needed

Muscles Strengthened

- outer thigh and buttocks (hip abductors)

Single-Joint ❖ Hip Adduction

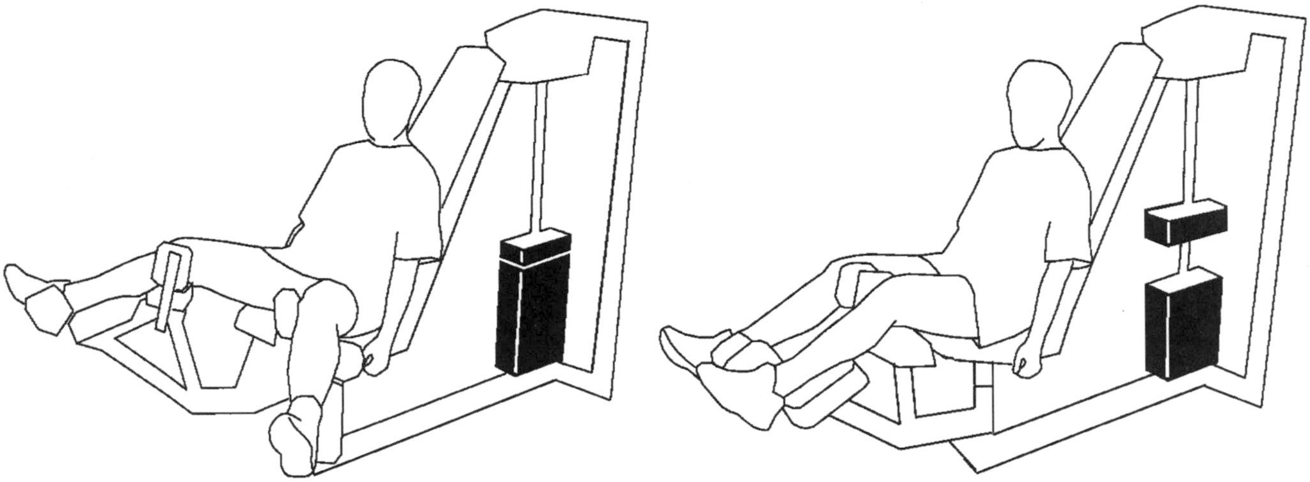

Hip Adduction—Machine

Starting Position

- seated on the seat provided
- head, lower back, and upper back in contact with the seat back
- legs comfortable, spread apart as wide as possible
- leg pads on the inside of the leg above the knee
- toes pointing straight up
- hands grasping the handles if provided
- on many machines it is possible to adjust how wide the legs will be allowed to spread

Finish Position & Movement

- in a controlled manner, bring the legs completely together
- hold the legs together briefly
- return to the starting position in a controlled manner
- toes remain pointing straight up at all times
- head, lower back, and upper back maintain contact with the seat back at all times

Common Technique Errors

- rocking the hips and lower back to help start the movement
- not spreading the legs as far as possible
- setting the machine so that the legs are spread too far, which can result in overstretching of the inner thigh muscles

Spotting & Safety

- no spotting is needed

Muscles Strengthened

- inner thigh and buttocks (hip adductors)

Single-Joint ❖ Hip Adduction

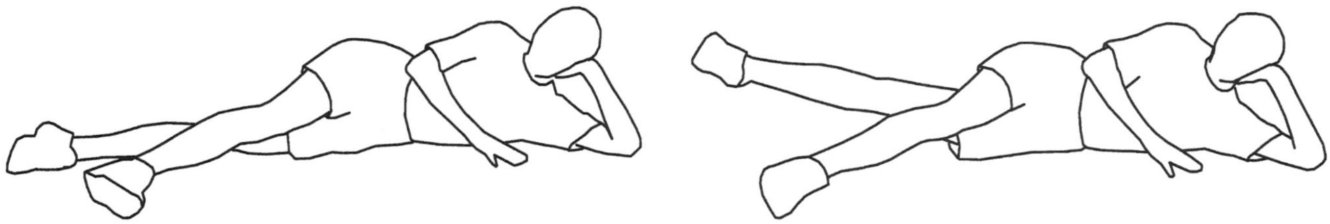

Hip Adduction—Lying

Starting Position

- lying on the side on the floor
- upper body supported by the arm nearest the floor
- legs are together but the top leg is slightly in front of the bottom leg
- toes pointing straight forward
- resistance can be added by attaching an ankle weight just above the knee

Finish Position & Movement

- in a controlled manner, raise the bottom leg as far as possible
- toes remain pointing straight forward at all times
- hold the highest leg position briefly
- return to the starting position in a controlled manner
- head, lower back, and upper back remain still at all times
- after completing the desired number of repetitions, switch legs

Common Technique Errors

- rocking the hips and lower back to help start the movement
- not raising the bottom leg as far as possible
- not keeping the toes pointing forward

Spotting & Safety

- no spotting is needed

Muscles Strengthened

- inner thigh and buttocks (hip adductors)

Single-Joint ❖ Gluteals

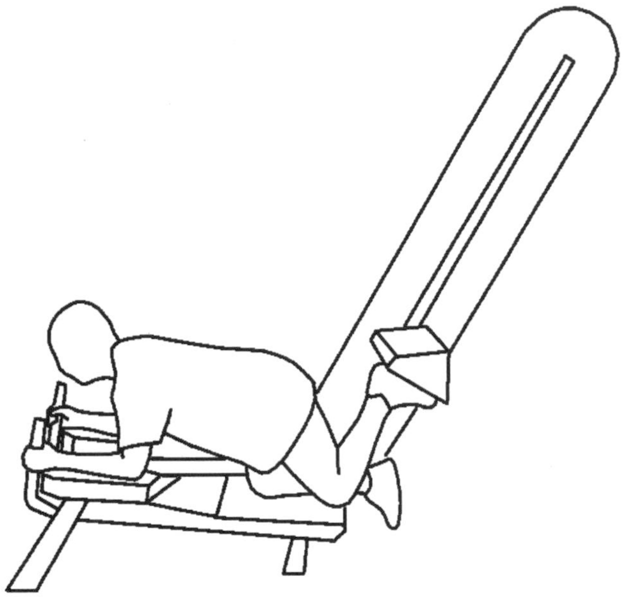

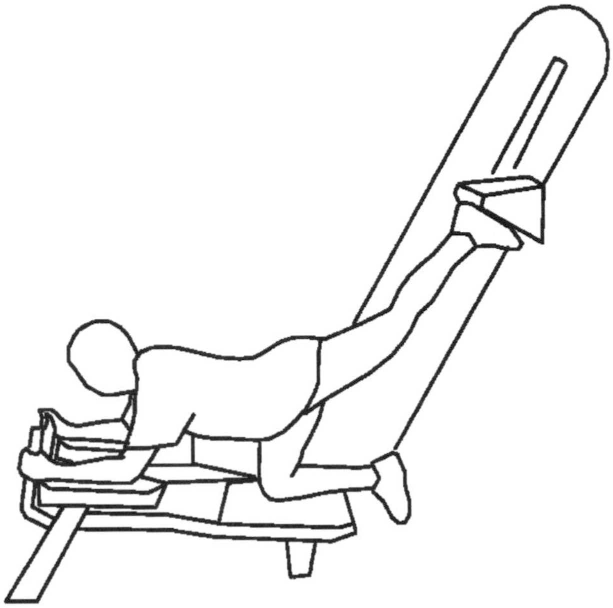

Butt Blaster

Starting Position

- kneeling on one knee
- one foot flat against the foot plate
- forearms on the pads provided and hands grasping the handles
- head in line with the rest of the back

Finish Position & Movement

- in a controlled manner, push the foot plate up as far as possible
- the foot remains flat on the foot plate at all times
- hold the highest position briefly
- return to the starting position in a controlled manner
- after completing the desired number of repetitions, switch legs

Common Technique Errors

- rocking the hips and lower back side to side to help start the movement
- not pushing the foot plate as high as possible

Spotting & Safety

- no spotting is needed

Muscles Strengthened

- buttocks (gluteals) and hamstrings

Single-Joint ❖ Gluteals

Dumbbell Butt Blaster

Starting Position

- kneeling on the floor
- a dumbbell held behind one knee
- head in line with the rest of the back

Finish Position & Movement

- in a controlled manner, raise the upper leg holding the dumbbell up and back as far as possible
- the knee must remain bent in order to hold the dumbbell
- hold the highest position briefly
- return to the starting position in a controlled manner
- after completing the desired number of repetitions, switch legs

Common Technique Errors

- rocking the hips and lower back side to side to help start the movement
- not raising the leg as high as possible

Spotting & Safety

- no spotting is needed

Muscles Strengthened

- buttocks (gluteals) and hamstrings

Single-Joint ❖ Calf

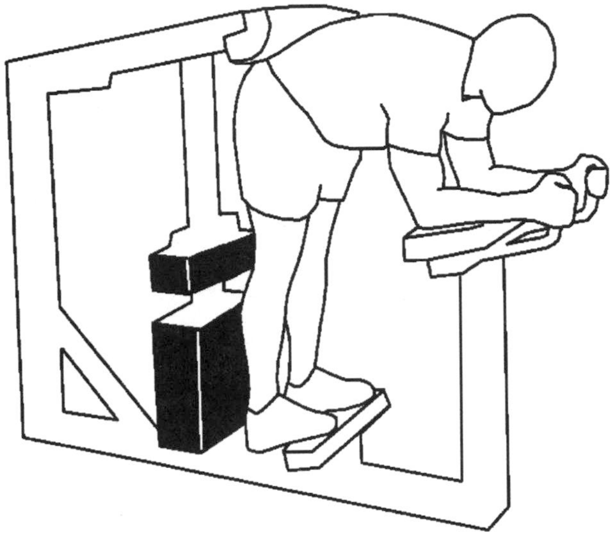

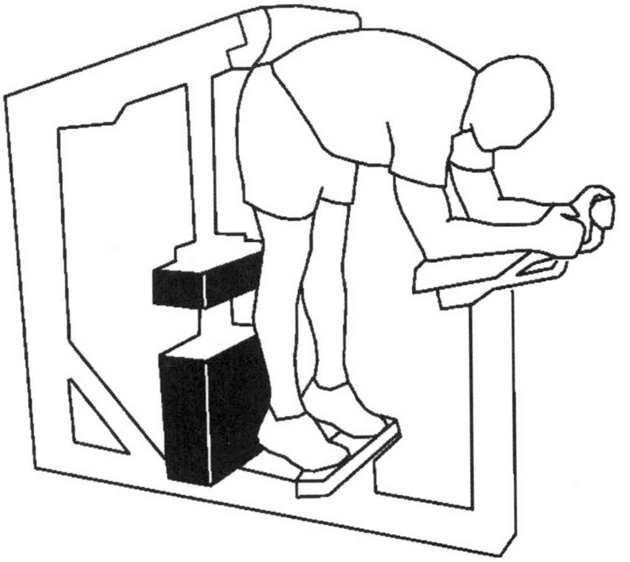

Calf Raise—Donkey—Toes Pointing Straight Forward

Variations

Toes Pointing In

Toes Pointing Out

Starting Position

- standing with feet hip width or slightly wider apart
- balls of the feet on the platform provided and heels as low as possible
- toes pointing straight forward
- hip pad on the hips and not on the lower back
- some older machines have a belt that goes around the waist and rests on the hips instead of a pad
- knees straight but not locked
- hands and/or arms resting on the handles or pad provided
- hips bent and torso leaning forward
- if possible, adjust the height of the hip pad to allow for full range of motion, with full stretch on the calf muscles in the start position and standing on toes as high as possible in the finish position

Finish Position & Movement

- in a controlled manner, contract the calves and stand on the toes as high as possible
- briefly hold the highest position
- return to the starting position in a controlled manner

Single-Joint ❖ Calf

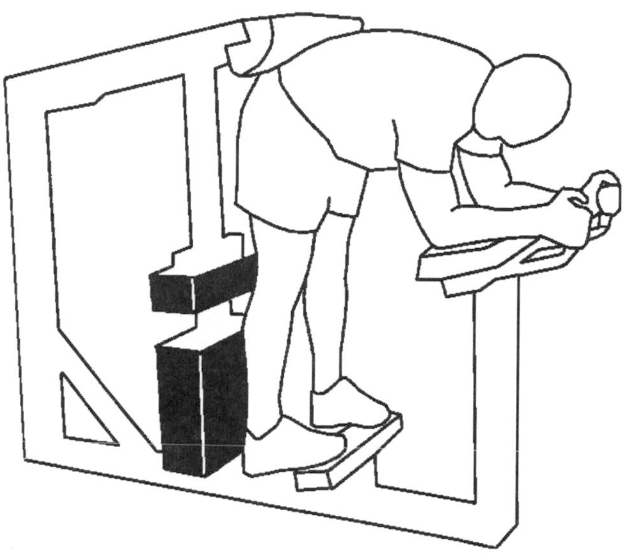

Calf Raise—Donkey—Toes Pointing In

Starting Position

same as for donkey calf raise with the toes pointing straight forward except:

- toes pointing in

Finish Position & Movement

same as for donkey calf raise with the toes pointing straight forward except:

- toes remain pointing in at all times

Single-Joint ❖ Calf

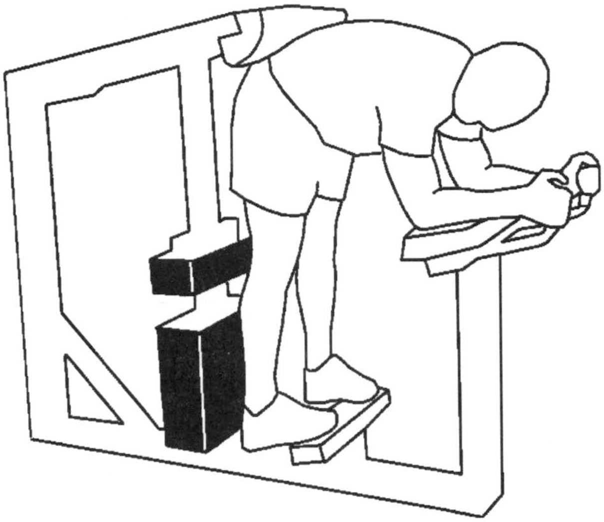

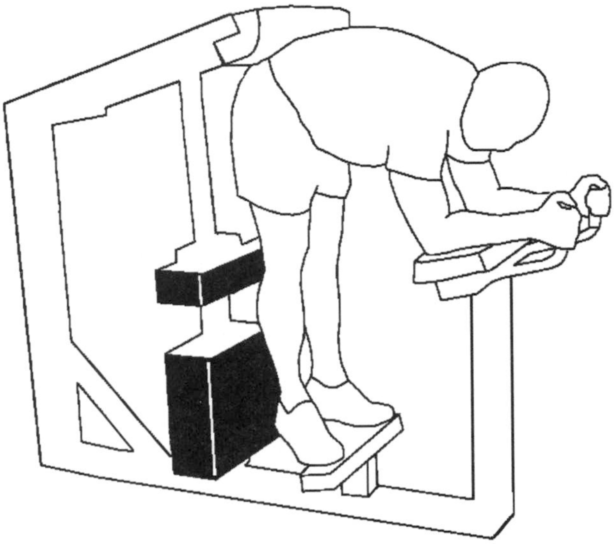

Calf Raise—Donkey—Toes Pointing Out

Starting Position

same as for donkey calf raise with the toes pointing straight forward except:

- toes pointing out

Finish Position & Movement

same as for donkey calf raise with the toes pointing straight forward except:

- toes remain pointing out at all times

Common Technique Errors

Toes Pointing Straight Forward, Toes Pointing In, and Toes Pointing Out

- not starting from as low of a heel position as possible
- not standing on the toes as high as possible

Spotting & Safety

Toes Pointing Straight Forward, Toes Pointing In, and Toes Pointing Out

- no spotting is needed
- make sure the toes do not slip off the platform

Muscles Strengthened

Toes Pointing Straight Forward, Toes Pointing In, and Toes Pointing Out

- calves (soleus and gastrocnemius)

Toes Pointing In

- trains especially the inside area of the gastrocnemius (medial head of gastrocnemius)

Toes Pointing Out

- trains especially the outside area of the gastrocnemius (lateral head of gastrocnemius)

Single-Joint ❖ Calf

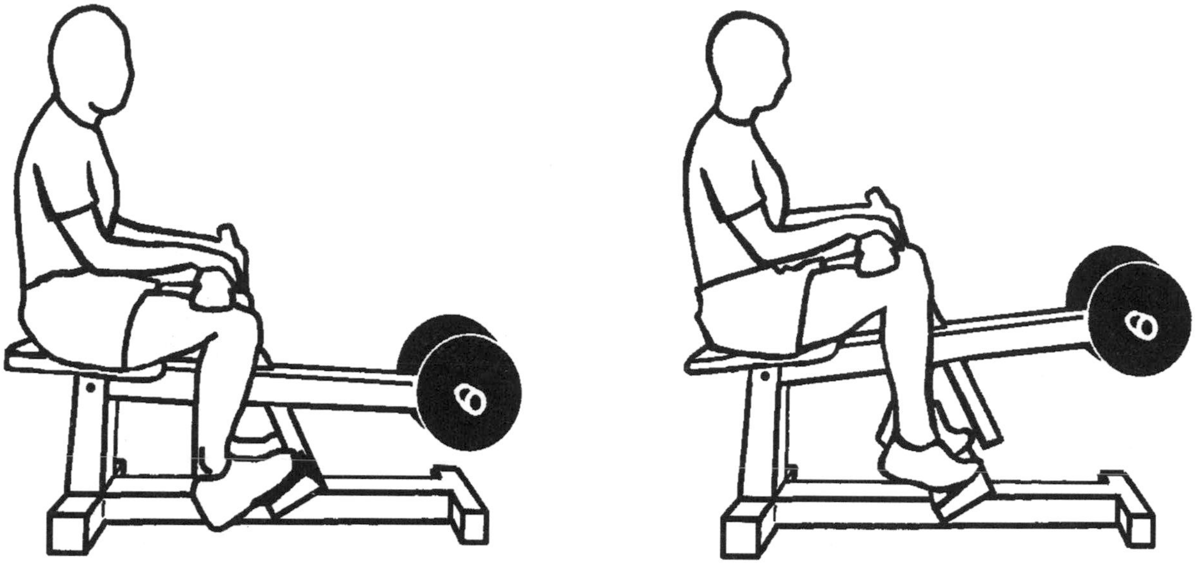

Calf Raise—Seated

Starting Position

- seated with feet hip width or slightly wider apart
- toes pointing directly forward, in, or out; toe position makes no difference to muscle use, so use whatever toe position is most comfortable
- ball of the feet on the platform provided and heels as low as possible
- torso upright and knees at about a 90 degree angle
- pads resting on the thigh just above the knees
- hands grasping the handles provided
- if possible, adjust the height of the thigh pads to allow for full range of motion, with a full stretch on calve muscles in the start position and standing on toes as high as possible in the finish position
- the machines have a way, usually a lever of some type, to place the weight on the calves and to remove the weight when a set is finished

Finish Position & Movement

- in a controlled manner, contract the calves and rise onto the toes as high as possible
- briefly hold the highest position
- return to the starting position in a controlled manner

Common Technique Errors

- not starting from as low of a heel position as possible
- not standing on the toes as high as possible

Spotting & Safety

- no spotting is needed
- make sure the toes do not slip off the platform

Muscles Strengthened

- calf area, especially the soleus
- toe position pointing in, out, or forward does not change muscle use in this exercise

Single-Joint ❖ Calf

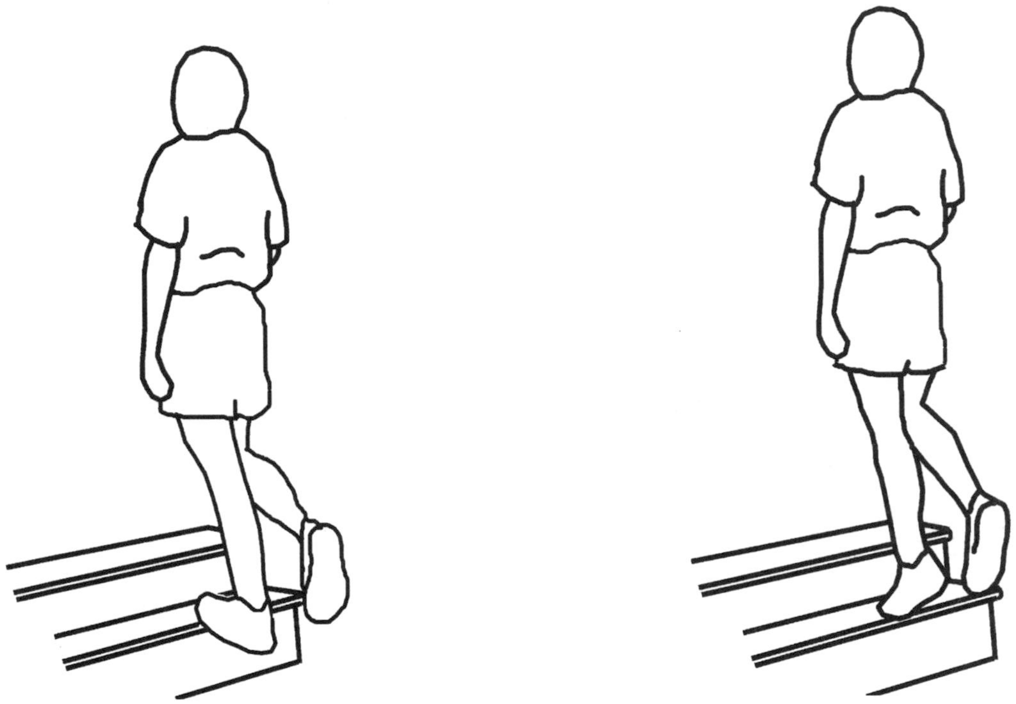

Standing Calf Raise—Standing—Body Weight with One Leg

Starting Position

- standing on one leg
- ball of the feet on a platform (such as a step) with the heel as low as possible
- knee straight but not locked
- one or both hands grasping something for balance, such as a handrail by the steps
- torso upright
- the exercise can be performed using body weight
- weight can be added by holding a dumbbell in one hand

Finish Position & Movement

- in a controlled manner, contract the calf and stand on the toes as high as possible
- briefly hold the highest position
- return to the starting position in a controlled manner
- after the desired number of repetitions, switch legs

Common Technique Errors

- not starting from as low of a heel position as possible
- not standing on the toes as high as possible

Spotting & Safety

- no spotting is needed
- make sure the toes do not slip off the platform

Muscles Strengthened

- entire calf (soleus and both heads of the gastrocnemius)

Single-Joint ❖ Calf

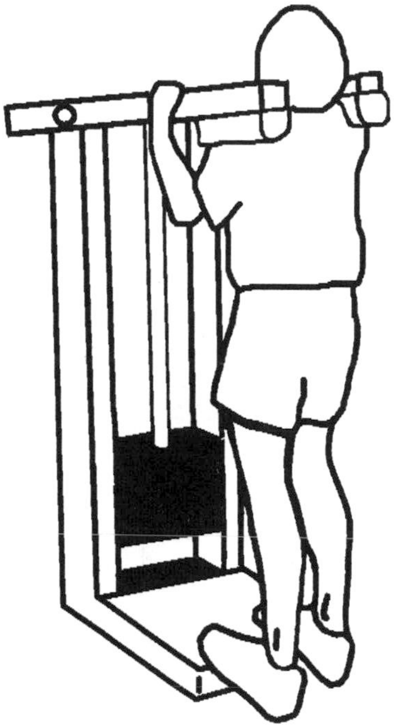

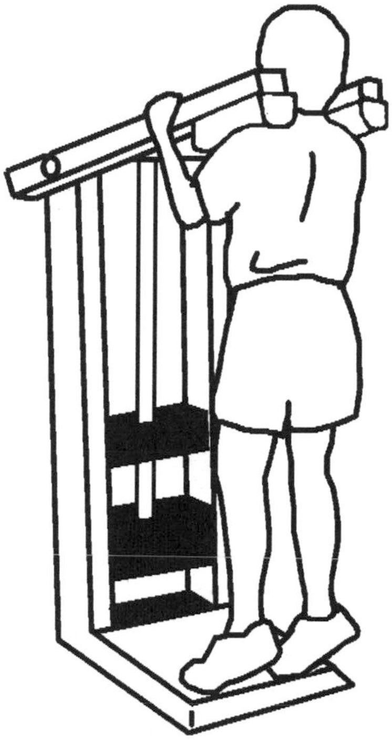

Standing Calf Raise—Machine—Toes Pointing Forward

Variations

Toes Pointing In

Toes Pointing Out

Starting Position

- standing with feet hip width or slightly wider apart
- toes pointing directly forward
- ball of the feet on the platform provided and heels as low as possible
- torso upright and shoulder pads on the shoulders
- knees straight but not locked
- hands are grasping the handles provided
- if possible, adjust the height of the shoulder pads to allow for full range of motion, with the heels as low as possible in the starting position and standing on toes as high as possible in the finish position

Finish Position & Movement

- in a controlled manner, contract the calves and stand on the toes as high as possible
- briefly hold the highest position
- return to the starting position in a controlled manner

Single-Joint ❖ Calf

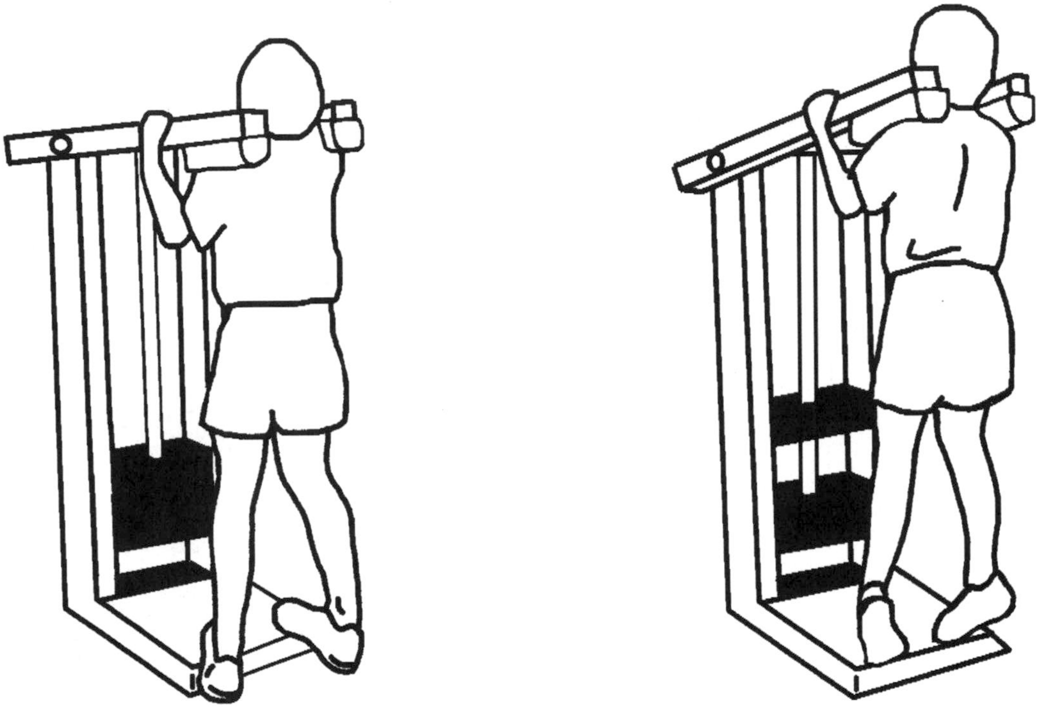

Standing Calf Raise—Machine—Toes Pointing In

Starting Position

same as for standing calf raise with the toes pointing forward except:

- toes pointing in

Finish Position & Movement

same as for standing calf raise with the toes pointing forward except:

- toes pointing in at all times

Single-Joint ❖ Calf

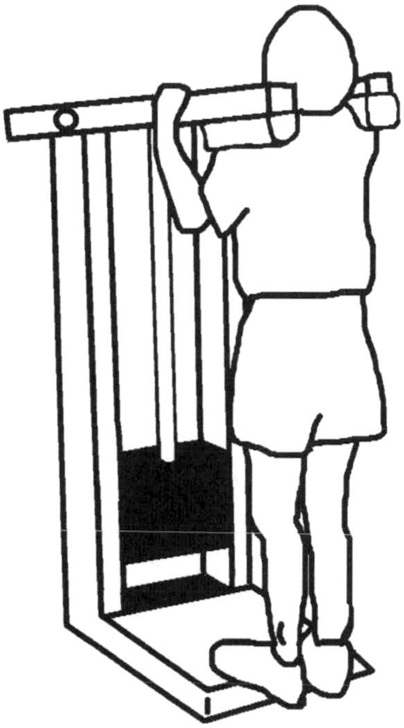

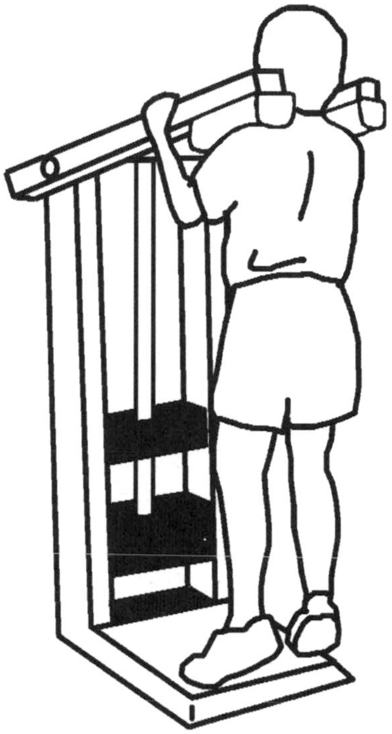

Standing Calf Raise—Machine—Toes Pointing Out

Starting Position

same as for standing calf raise with the toes pointing forward except:

- toes pointing out

Finish Position & Movement

same as for standing calf raise with the toes pointing forward except:

- toes pointing out at all times

Common Technique Errors

Toes Pointing Forward, Toes Pointing In, and Toes Pointing Out

- not starting from as low of a heel position as possible
- not standing on the toes as high as possible

Spotting & Safety

Toes Pointing Forward, Toes Pointing In, and Toes Pointing Out

- no spotting is needed
- make sure the toes do not slip off the platform

Muscles Strengthened

Toes Pointing Forward, Toes Pointing In, and Toes Pointing Out

- entire calf area (soleus and gastrocnemius)

Toes Pointing In

- trains especially the inside area of the gastrocnemius (medial head of gastrocnemius)

Toes Pointing Out

- trains especially the outside area of the gastrocnemius (lateral head of gastrocnemius)

Single-Joint ❖ Lower Back

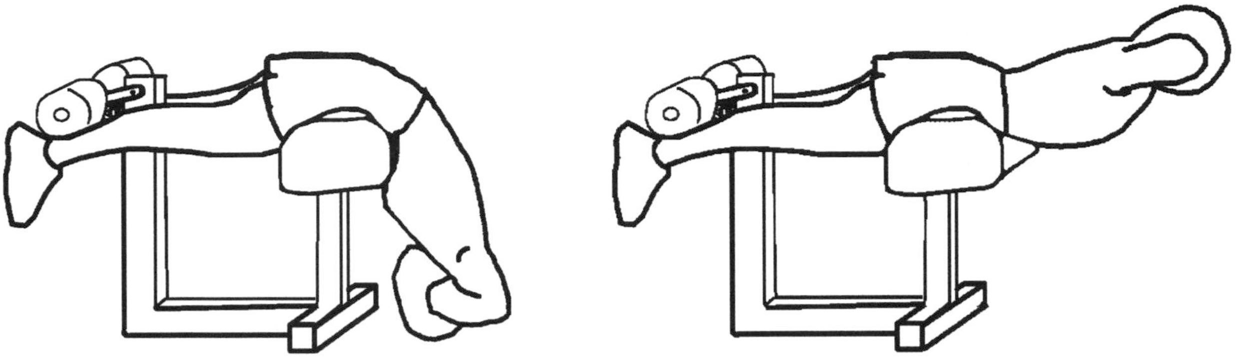

Back Extension

Starting Position

- lying face down with the hips on the pad and the ankles hooked below the pads provided
- hips just over the front edge of the pad to allow easy movement
- knees slightly bent
- if possible, adjust the distance between the ankle and hip pads so the hips are just off of the pad
- if possible, adjust the height of the ankle pads so that the ankles are slightly below the hip pad
- torso hanging down so that the legs and torso form a 90 degree angle
- arms crossed in front of chest
- to make the exercise more difficult, the hands can be clasped behind the head
- to add resistance, a weight can be held in front of the chest

Finish Position & Movement

- in a controlled manner, raise the torso upward until it is parallel to the floor
- briefly hold the parallel-to-floor position
- return to the starting position in a controlled manner

Common Technique Errors

- swinging the torso to help start the movement
- raising the torso above the parallel-to-floor position can place strain on the lower back

Spotting & Safety

- no spotter is needed

Muscles Strengthened

- lower back area (lumbar extensors)

Single-Joint ❖ Lower Back

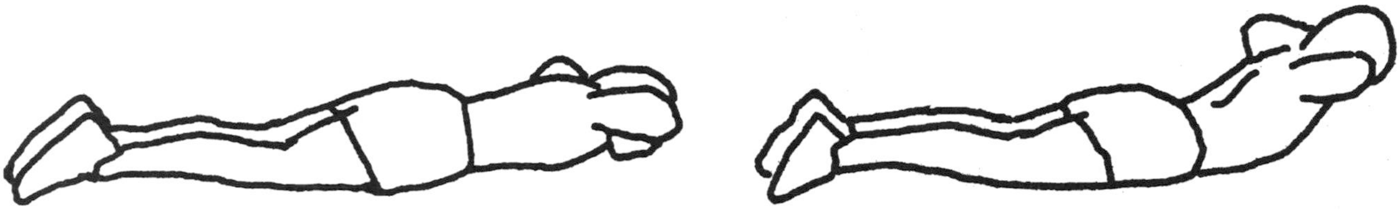

Back Extension—Lying

Starting Position

- lying on the stomach flat on the floor
- hands clasped behind the head
- chin almost touching floor
- a partner may hold the lower body down by placing his or her hands just above the knees
- to add resistance, a weight plate can be held behind the lower neck and upper back area

Finish Position & Movement

- in a controlled manner, raise the torso several inches off the floor
- briefly hold the highest position
- return to the starting position in a controlled manner

Common Technique Errors

- holding a weight plate behind the head instead of the lower neck can place strain on the neck

Spotting & Safety

- no spotter is needed

Muscles Strengthened

- lower back area (lumbar extensors)

Single-Joint ❖ Lower Back

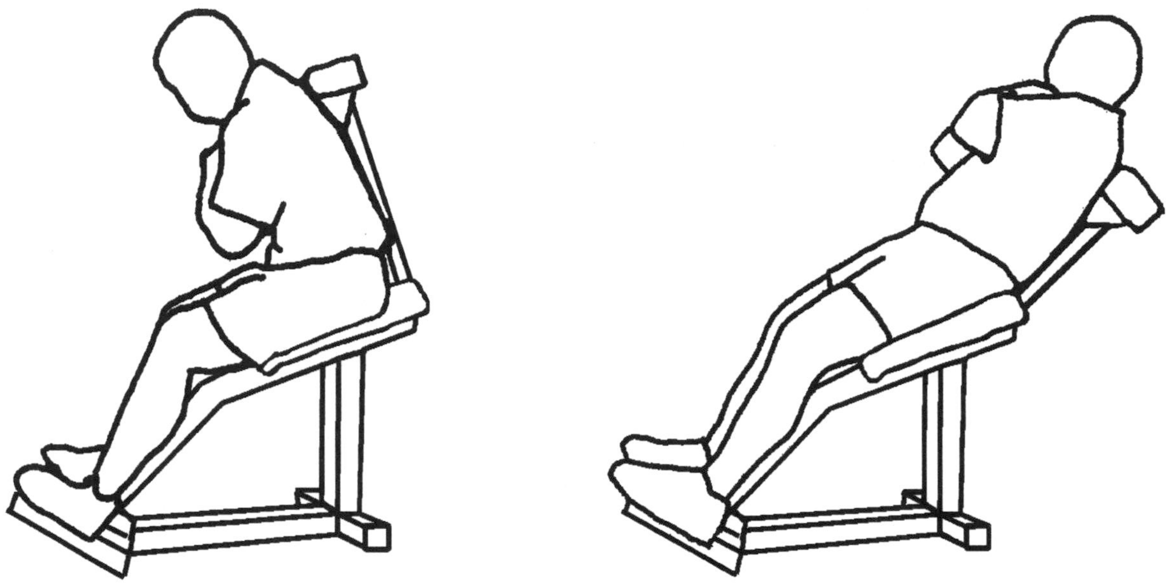

Back Extension—Machine

Starting Position

- normally seated with a pad that applies resistance on the upper back area
- securely fasten the seat belt around the hips
- if possible, adjust the seat height and make other adjustments for proper equipment fit
- the feet should be flat on the floor or on the platform provided on the machine

Finish Position & Movement

- in a controlled manner, push back on the upper back pad and straighten the lower back as far as possible
- briefly hold the position with the back straightened as much as possible
- return to the starting position in a controlled manner

Common Technique Errors

- swinging the torso to help start the movement

Spotting & Safety

- no spotter is needed

Muscles Strengthened

- lower back area (lumbar extensors)

Single-Joint ❖ Lower Back

Dead Lift—Straight Legged

Starting Position

- pick barbell up as if doing a dead lift (see p. 116)
- stand erect, feet hip width or slightly wider apart, a slight bend in the knees and head upright
- barbell held at arm's length and touching the thighs
- barbell held with a grip that is shoulder width or slightly wider
- either two overhand grips (palms facing the shins) or a mixed grip, one overhand grip and one underhand (palm facing forward), can be used
- body weight over the mid-foot area
- the entire back straight and stiff

Finish Position & Movement

- keeping the back straight, slowly bend over at the waist until the barbell almost touches the floor (one inch or less off the floor)
- do not bend the lower back but rotate around your hip joints
- if done correctly, the buttocks will raise slightly and you will feel a stretch on the hamstrings
- body weight should be kept over the center of the foot or rear foot during the lift
- neck is in line with the rest of the back
- after almost touching the floor with the barbell, return to starting position in a controlled manner

Common Technique Errors

- not keeping the back straight and stiff
- bouncing the barbell off the floor in preparation for the next repetition

Spotting & Safety

- no spotters are needed

Muscles Strengthened

- lower back area (lumbar extensors) and hamstrings

Single-Joint ❖ Lower Back

Good Mornings

Starting Position

starting position is similar to the starting position for a back squat (see p. 114)

- stand erect, feet hip width or slightly wider apart and a slight bend in the knees
- barbell resting on the spines of the shoulder blades (not on the neck)
- hands grasp the bar wider than shoulder width using an overhand grip and help in supporting and balancing the barbell
- head upright

Finish Position & Movement

- keeping the lower back straight, in a controlled manner, bend forward from the waist
- do not bend the lower back but rotate around your hip joints
- if done properly, buttocks will raise slightly and you will feel a stretch on the hamstring muscles
- bend forward until the torso is parallel to the floor
- briefly hold the parallel-to-floor position
- return to the starting position

Common Technique Errors

- placing the barbell too high on the shoulders, thereby placing pressure on the neck
- going past the parallel-to-floor position places excessive stress on the lower back
- not having the barbell centered on the shoulders

Spotting & Safety

- the barbell can be taken off a power rack
- two spotters (one at each end of the barbell) can be used

Muscles Strengthened

- lower back area (lumbar extensors)

Single-Joint ❖ Lower Back

Superhero

Starting Position

- lying on the stomach, flat on the floor
- arms out in front of the shoulders

Finish Position & Movement

- in a controlled manner, raise the torso and the legs off the floor several inches
- briefly hold the highest position
- return to the starting position in a controlled manner

Common Technique Errors

- swinging the arms and legs and using momentum to get the torso and legs off the floor

Spotting & Safety

- no spotter is needed

Muscles Strengthened

- lower back area (lumbar extensors)

Single-Joint ❖ Abdominals

Bent Leg Sit-Up

Variation

Twisting Bent Leg Sit-Up

Starting Position

- lying on the back on the floor
- knees bent, with the feet flat on the floor and the heels about six inches from the buttocks
- arms are crossed over the chest
- to make the exercise more difficult, the ears may be clasped with the fingers or a weight plate held on the chest
- an incline sit-up board may also be used to increase the resistance by increasing the incline of the board
- an incline sit-up board has pads under which the feet can be hooked to hold them down

Finish Position & Movement

- keeping the hips on the floor, in a controlled manner, raise the torso toward the knees
- the back is kept straight as the torso is raised
- the torso is raised until the shoulders are several inches off the floor
- hold the highest position briefly, and return to the starting position in a controlled manner

Single-Joint ❖ Abdominals

Twisting Bent Leg Sit-Up

Starting Position

same as for a bent leg sit-up

Finish Position & Movement

similar to a bent leg sit-up except:

- after raising the torso to the highest position, the lifter twists slightly to the left and then to the right

Common Technique Errors

Bent Leg Sit-Up and Twisting Bent Leg Sit-Up

- moving the arms to help start the movement
- clasping the hands behind the head and pulling with the arms to help raise the torso can place stress on the neck
- rocking the hips to help start the movement

Spotting & Safety

Bent Leg Sit-Up and Twisting Bent Leg Sit-Up

- no spotting is needed
- an assistant can hold the feet on the floor by placing his or her hands on the feet and ankles of the lifter

Muscles Strengthened

Bent Leg Sit-Up and Twisting Bent Leg Sit-Up

- abdominal area
- bent leg sit-ups allow more use of the hip flexors than do crunches

Twisting Bent Leg Sit-Up

- also trains the sides of the abdominal area (obliques)

Single-Joint ❖ Abdominals

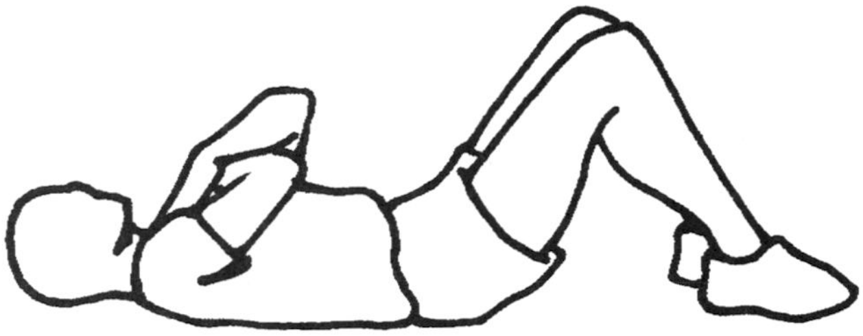

CRUNCH

Variation

Twisting Crunch

Starting Position

- lying on the back on the floor
- knees bent, with the feet flat on the floor and the heels about six inches from the buttocks
- arms crossed over the chest
- to make the exercise more difficult, the ears may be clasped with the fingers or a weight plate held on the chest

Finish Position & Movement

- keeping the hips on the floor, in a controlled manner, raise the torso toward the knees
- torso is raised by rounding the entire back
- torso is raised enough so that the shoulder blades are several inches off the floor
- hold the highest position briefly, and return to the starting position in a controlled manner
- the arms should remain stationary throughout the exercise motion

Single-Joint ❖ Abdominals

Twisting Crunch

Starting Position

same as for a crunch

Finish Position & Movement

same as for a crunch except:

- after raising the torso to the highest position, the lifter twists slightly to the left and then to the right

Common Technique Errors

Crunch and Twisting Crunch

- moving the arms to help start the movement
- clasping the hands behind the head and pulling with the arms to help raise the torso can place stress on the neck
- rocking the hips to help start the movement

Twisting Crunch

- twisting while the shoulders are still on the floor
- twisting on the way up instead of while in the highest position

Spotting & Safety

Crunch and Twisting Crunch

- no spotting is needed

Muscles Strengthened

Crunch and Twisting Crunch

- abdominal area

Twisting Crunch

- emphasizes the sides of the abdominal area (obliques)

Single-Joint ❖ Abdominals

Abdominal Machine

Starting Position

- sitting on the machine's seat
- back flat against the back of the seat
- feet flat on the floor
- hands grasping the handles behind the head or arms crossed over the pad provided
- if possible, adjust the machine for proper fit

Finish Position & Movement

- keeping the feet flat on the floor, in a controlled manner, pull the ribs toward the thighs as when doing a crunch
- return to the starting position in a controlled manner

Common Technique Errors

- moving the arms to help start the movement
- rocking the hips to help start the movement

Spotting & Safety

- no spotting is needed

Muscles Strengthened

- abdominal area

Chapter *Nine*

Sample Programs

Sample programs are very helpful to anyone beginning a strength training program—they provide examples for modeling your own program. Use the information presented in all the chapters to create a program that fits your needs and goals. If you do not have a certain piece of weight training equipment or do not wish to do a certain exercise, substitute an exercise for the same muscle group into the program. Do not be afraid to experiment a little with your program.

It is very easy to overdo it when you first start a program and to wind up very sore. Be sure to give yourself time to get used to the stress of weight training. For example, only do one set of each exercise for several weeks before you add additional sets. Each time you add a set, give yourself several more weeks before you add another set. This type of adjustment period should be used whenever you make any change, such as increasing the number of sessions per week, in your program.

You will make very good gains during the first several weeks of training. After this, gains will slow down, and the longer you train and the better the shape you get into, the more time it will take to see a gain in fitness. So do not expect continual large gains after acquiring a degree of good fitness. After you are in good shape, it is necessary to use all the information in this book to vary your training program on a regular basis. This will help ensure long-term gains in fitness.

Total Body Circuit

Circuit training is performing one set of an exercise and then moving on to the next exercise, with only a short rest period between exercises. If more than one set of an exercise is to be done, one set for every exercise is done and then the circuit is repeated. It is the best type of weight training if the major goal of the weight training program is to increase aerobic fitness. Remember, however, that traditional aerobic training will increase cardiovascular endurance three to five times more than circuit weight training will.

Format

Repetitions/Set: 12 to 15

Resistance: last few repetitions per set are difficult

Sets: 1 to 3

Exercise Order: initially alternating exercises for body parts, perform one set of an exercise and then move on to the next exercise until one set of each exercise is performed

Rest Periods: initially 1 minute

Equipment: machines or free weights or a combination of both; due to the need for short rest periods, machines on which it is easy to adjust the resistance are a good choice

Exercises: (perform exercises in the order listed)

- leg press or squat
- bench press or chest press
- knee curl
- overhead press
- knee extension
- incline press
- standing calf raise
- lat pull-down
- crunch
- seated row or bent-over row (dumbbells)
- machine or EZ curl bar arm curl

Training Variations

Exercise Choice: add exercises to train a desired muscle group—for example, women may want to add hip adduction and abduction; substitute an exercise for the same muscle group—for example, substitute the seated calf raise for the standing calf raise

Exercise Order: gradually go to a stacked exercise order

Sets: gradually increase to 2 and then 3 complete circuits if desired; perform 2 or 3 sets of only specific exercises to emphasize a muscle group—for example do 2 additional sets of leg press and knee extension at the end of the circuit to emphasize the quadriceps

Rest Periods: gradually shorten to 30 seconds

Male Cycled Total Body Program: Bench Press & Squat

This is a program emphasizing bench press and leg press or squat ability. It is composed of four one-month cycles or programs. After completing the four months of training, the program is repeated. Throughout this program, the volume of training is decreased by decreasing the total number of exercises and the number of repetitions per set, while intensity is increased. This will result in an increase in the maximal weight that can be lifted in the bench press and squat or leg press. It is also possible to use each one-month program individually, if any of the months' goals are your goals. If peaking maximal bench press or squat ability is not a major training goal, you can elect not to do the strength phase training month and do only the first three months of training and then repeat them.

Base Size Phase

The goal of this month of training is to increase muscle size and endurance and to prepare the lifter for the upcoming training phases. If you are just beginning weight training, you may wish to do this program for six to eight weeks before going on to the next training phase.

Format

Repetitions/Set: 15 to 20

Resistance: last few repetitions per set are difficult

Sets: 1 to 3; initially 1 if just beginning weight training

Exercise Order: initially alternating exercises for body parts, perform all sets of an exercise and then move on to the next exercise

Rest Periods: initially 2 minutes, gradually decreasing to 1 minute as the phase progresses

Equipment: machines or free weights or a combination of both

Exercises: (initially perform in order listed)
- squat or leg press
- bench press
- knee curl
- incline press
- knee extension
- pec deck or dumbbell fly
- standing calf raise
- triceps push-down
- seated row
- crunch
- concentration curl

Training Variations

Exercise Choice: add an exercise for a muscle group needing emphasis

Exercise Order: gradually go to a stacked exercise order

Sets: if it is needed to shorten the training session, do 3 sets of the multi-joint exercises like the bench press, squat, and seated row and only 1 or 2 sets of the single-joint exercises

Rest Periods: gradually shorten to 1 minute, use 2 minutes between the squat or leg press and bench press and less than 2 minutes between the rest of the exercises

Size Phase

The major goal of this training month is to increase muscle size. As the rest periods are shortened, an increase in blood lactate, a by-product of anaerobic energy use, will occur. This will result in some discomfort, so listen to your body as you shorten the rest periods.

Format

Repetitions/Set: 12 to 15; use a lower number of repetitions for the bench press and squat or leg press

Resistance: last few repetitions per set are difficult

Sets: 2 to 3; use 3 sets for muscle groups needing emphasis, for example, use 3 sets for the squat or leg press and bench press only

Exercise Order: in general stacked exercise order, perform all sets of an exercise and then move on to the next exercise

Rest Periods: 1.5 to 1 minute

Equipment: machines or free weights or a combination of both

Exercises: (initially perform in order listed)
- squat or leg press
- bench press
- knee curl
- knee extension
- donkey or standing calf raise
- triceps push-down
- seated row
- standing arm curl (dumbbells)
- crunch or abdominal machine
- back extension

Training Variations

Exercise Choice: add an exercise for a weak muscle group

Exercise Order: do the bench press or leg press or squat first in the session, whichever you desire to emphasize; do all arm or leg training first in the session, whichever you desire to emphasize

Sets: do 3 sets only for the bench press or squat or leg press; do 3 sets for arm or leg training, whichever you desire to emphasize

Rest Periods: use 2 minutes between the bench press or squat and leg press so that you can use slightly greater resistance; gradually shorten all rest periods to 1 minute

Size and Strength Phase

The goals of this phase are to increase size and maximal strength. A secondary goal is to prepare the lifter for using heavier weights in the upcoming strength phase.

Format

Repetitions/Set: 8 to 10
Resistance: true repetition maximum weights for the number of repetitions done
Sets: 2 to 3; use 3 sets for muscle groups needing emphasis, for example, use 3 sets for the squat or leg press and bench press only
Exercise Order: in general, use a stacked exercise order; perform all sets of an exercise and then move on to the next exercise
Rest Periods: 1 to 2 minutes
Equipment: machines or free weights or a combination of both
Exercises: (initially perform in order listed)

- squat or leg press
- bench press
- knee curl
- knee extension
- bench press (dumbbells)
- incline or decline bench press
- dip
- seated row
- crunch or abdominal machine
- back extension

Training Variations

Exercise Choice: add an exercise for a muscle group needing emphasis
Exercise Order: do the bench press or leg press or squat first in the session, whichever you desire to emphasize; do all arm or leg training first in the session, whichever you desire to emphasize
Sets: do 3 sets only for the bench press or squat or leg press; do 3 sets for arm or leg training, whichever you desire to emphasize
Rest Periods: use 2 to 3 minutes between the bench press or squat and leg press so that you can use slightly greater resistance

Strength Phase

The major goal of this phase is to peak and express maximal strength in the bench press and leg press or squat. The volume of training is kept low by using predominantly multi-joint exercises. Intensity is at its highest during this phase of the four-month program.

Format

Repetitions/Set: 6 to 8
Resistance: true repetition maximum weights for the number of repetitions done
Sets: 2 to 3; use 3 sets for the squat or leg press and bench press only, use 3 sets for muscle groups needing emphasis
Exercise Order: squat or leg press and bench press first, then in general, use on stacked exercise order; perform all sets of an exercise and then move on to the next exercise
Rest Periods: 2 to 3 minutes
Equipment: machines or free weights or a combination of both
Exercises: (initially perform in order listed)

- squat or leg press
- bench press
- incline or decline press
- seated row
- crunch or abdominal machine

Training Variations

Exercise Choice: add an exercise for a muscle group needing emphasis
Exercise Order: do the bench press or leg press or squat first in the session, whichever you desire to emphasize
Sets: do 3 sets only for the bench press or squat or leg press

Rest Periods: use 3 minutes or longer between the bench press or squat and leg press so that you can use slightly greater resistance
Resistance & Repetitions: if desired, it is possible to do 2 to 3 reps per set for the bench press, squat, or leg press

Female Cycled Total Body Toning Program

This is a program emphasizing leg, hip, and abdominal areas, all common areas of interest for many women. It is composed of three one-month cycles or programs. After completing the three months of training, the program is repeated. Throughout this program, the volume of training is relatively high, while intensity moves from relatively low (18 to 20 reps per set) to moderately high (10 to 12 reps per set). This will result in a program that tones and shapes the body. It is also possible to use each one-month program individually, if any of the months' goals are your goals.

Base Toning Phase

The goal of this month of training is to tone the muscles, decrease the percentage of body fat, and prepare the lifter for the upcoming training phases. If you are just beginning weight training you may wish to do this program for six to eight weeks before going on to the next training phase.

Format

Repetitions/Set: 18 to 20
Resistance: last few repetitions per set are difficult
Sets: 1 to 3; initially 1 if just beginning weight training
Exercise Order: initially alternating exercises for body parts; perform all sets of an exercise and then move on to the next exercise
Rest Periods: initially 2 minutes, gradually decreasing to 1 minute as the phase progresses
Equipment: machines or free weights or a combination of both
Exercises: (initially perform in order listed)

leg press or lunge
bench press
knee curl
seated row
knee extension
triceps push-down
standing calf raise
machine arm curl
hip adduction
crunch
hip abduction
abdominal machine

Training Variations

Exercise Choice: add an exercise to emphasize a muscle group
Exercise Order: gradually go to a stacked exercise order
Sets: if it is needed to shorten the training session, do 3 sets of lower body and abdominal exercises and only 1 or 2 sets of upper body exercises
Rest Periods: gradually shorten to 1 minute

Toning Phase

The major goal of this training month is to tone the muscles, lower the percentage of body fat, and increase strength. As the rest periods are shortened, an increase in blood lactate, a by-product of anaerobic energy use, will occur. This will result in some discomfort, so listen to your body as you shorten the rest periods.

Format

Repetitions/Set: 12 to 15
Resistance: last few repetitions per set are difficult

Sets: 2 to 3; use 3 sets for muscle groups needing emphasis
Exercise Order: in general, use a stacked exercise order; perform all sets of an exercise and then move on to the next exercise
Rest Periods: 1.5 to 1 minute
Equipment: machines or free weights or a combination of both
Exercises: (initially perform in order listed)

- leg press
- butt blaster
- knee extension
- donkey calf raise
- hip adduction
- hip abduction
- chest press
- seated row or bent-over row (dumbbells)
- standing arm curl (EZ curl bar)
- triceps push-down
- twisting crunch
- abdominal machine

Training Variations

Exercise Choice: add an exercise to emphasize a muscle group; delete a single-joint exercise for a muscle group not needing emphasis
Exercise Order: do upper or lower body training first, whichever you desire to emphasize; use an alternating order, if needed, for added rest between exercises for the same body part
Sets: do 3 sets of exercises for muscle groups needing emphasis
Rest Periods: gradually shorten all rest periods to 1 minute

Toning and Strength Phase

The goals of this phase are to tone and increase strength.

Format

Repetitions/Set: 8 to 10
Resistance: use true repetition maximum weights for the desired number of repetitions per set
Sets: 2 to 3
Exercise Order: in general, use a stacked exercise order; perform all sets of an exercise and then move on to the next exercise
Rest Periods: 1 to 2 minutes
Equipment: machines or free weights or a combination of both
Exercises: (initially perform in order listed)

- leg press
- knee curl
- knee extension
- standing calf raise
- chest or bench press
- lat pull-down
- dumbbell arm curl
- triceps kickback (dumbells)
- abdominal machine

Training Variations

Exercise Choice: add an exercise to emphasize a muscle group
Exercise Order: do all arm or leg training first in session, whichever you desire to emphasize
Sets: do 3 sets of exercises training the muscle groups needing emphasis
Rest Periods: use 2 minutes between exercises for which you desire to have increased strength

Body-Part Program

With a body-part program, each training session is dedicated solely to certain body parts or muscle groups. Body-part programs are arranged so that each body part is trained once every four to seven days. Many variations of body-part programs can be developed using different numbers of sessions per week, repetitions per set, and sets. These types of programs were started by bodybuilders but now have been adapted for use for total body fitness. Bodybuilders utilize body-part programs so that a large volume of training can be performed by the body part being trained in each session. After having performed a large volume of training, the body part is allowed to recover for the next three days or longer. Bodybuilders believe that this will result in greater muscle size gains than with other types of programs.

Bodybuilders do three or more exercises for a body part per session. In general, all exercises are performed for multiple sets. So a large volume of training is actually performed by the body part. In general, bodybuilders carry all sets done to momentary failure. The programs are successful because of the large volume of training performed and carrying sets to momentary failure. You cannot take a body-part program and drastically reduce the number of exercises and sets done and expect it to be successful. The program is built on the idea that after a large volume of training and thus such a stressful session, multiple recovery days are needed before the next session for that body part. For general fitness, body-part programs do offer the advantage of relatively short duration sessions, but if a body part is to be trained once a week, almost daily sessions are required. These factors must be remembered if you are going to use a body-part program.

Format

Repetitions/Set: 8 to 10

Resistance: last few repetitions per set are very difficult

Sets: 3; initially 1 to 2 if just beginning to use a body-part program

Exercise Order: stacked order; perform all sets of an exercise before moving on to the next exercise

Rest Periods: initially 2 minutes, gradually decreasing to 1 minute

Equipment: machines or free weights or a combination of both

Exercises: (perform in the order listed)

Monday: chest and biceps
bench press (barbell) or chest press
incline press (dumbells or machine)
dumbbell fly or pec deck
arm curl (EZ curl bar or machine)
concentration curl or hammer curl

Tuesday: quadriceps and calves
squat
leg press
knee extension
standing calf raise
seated calf raise

Wednesday: trapeziuses and abdominals
shoulder shrug (barbell or machine)
shoulder shrug (dumbbells)
crunch (20 reps per set)
abdominal machine (20 reps per set)

Thursday: triceps and shoulders
triceps push-down or triceps extension (machine)
triceps extension (dumbbells)
overhead press (dumbbells or machine)
lateral shoulder raise (dumbbells or machine)

Friday: back and hamstrings
lat pull-down
seated or T-bar row
dead lift
knee curls (seated or lying)

Saturday and Sunday: no training

Training Variations

Exercise Choice: add exercises to emphasize a muscle group or as a substitute for exercises already in the program

Exercise Order: alternate on a set basis two exercises for the same muscle group or body part (i.e.,

super set), for example, alternate between the triceps push-down and dumbbell triceps extension
Sets: add sets to exercises in which an emphasis is desired
Rest Periods: use 2 minutes between exercises with which you desire to emphasize strength increases

BODY WEIGHT PROGRAM

Body weight exercises require little or no equipment; therefore, they can be done virtually anywhere. This makes them ideal for an at-home or on-the-road program. Not all body weight exercises are, however, easy to do. For example, pull-ups are a body weight exercise, and many people cannot do even one pull-up. Body weight is used as the resistance to be moved with a body weight exercise. Changing the resistance used is therefore not an easy proposition for some body weight exercises because it entails losing weight. It is, however, possible to hold a common object, like a book, to add some resistance to a body weight exercise. It is also possible to hold dumbbells, if available, to add resistance to some body weight exercises.

Format

Repetitions/Set: 15 to 20 or more
Resistance: body weight
Sets: 1 to 3; use 3 sets for muscle groups needing emphasis
Exercise Order: alternating order initially; when ciruit training, perform all sets of an exercise and then move on to the next exercise
Rest Periods: 1.5 to 1 minute
Equipment: a book, etc., or dumbbells can be used to add resistance if needed for some exercises
Exercises: (initially perform in order listed)

- squat
- push-up
- lunge
- self-resisted arm curl (use opposite arm to apply resistance in an arm curl motion)
- crunch
- back extension (lying)
- pull-up

Training Variations

Exercise Choice: use added weight in the form of a book, etc., or dumbbells if needed
Exercise Order: stack lower body exercises
Sets: add sets to exercises for which an emphasis is desired
Rest Periods: as with circuit weight training, there should be little or no rest between exercises

You now are ready to develop an individualized training program that fits exactly your needs and goals. After all, no one knows better than you what your fitness desires are. Good luck and good training.